PREFACE

Welcome to Church Stretton and South Sh beauty. Church Stretton, the natural "cen hills, gets its name from the Roman Ro forms the A49 by-pass. Church Stret The Church which stands near the Rom soft shale rock overlaid with boulder c oldest rocks in Britain Pre-Cambrian volc feet thick (from top to bottom). The Long Mynd, the most popular of the Stretton Hills, is 10 miles long by 4 miles wide at its widest point, and covers 70 square miles of which over 5000 acres are in the care of the National Trust.

ABOUT THIS BOOK: first published in 1970 this guide was entirely rewritten and revised for the 1994 season and four entirely new walks have been introduced for this 1999 edition. Every walk is most meticulously researched and mapped personally by the author who has been walking this area for the past 42 years.

The book is divided into three sections (1) walks in the Stretton Hills which start from the town itself (2) walks across the hills to surrounding villages, (3) walks elsewhere in the South Shropshire Area. With the aid of this book and its wide diversity of carefully selected walks the reader will take in a wide variety of different types of countryside.

Most of the maps are drawn to scale. Each map is drawn with regard to what you will see on the walk, position of trees, gates,buildings, etc. Always bear in mind, however, that in the countryside things are liable to change, hedgerows may be grubbed out, trees cut down or even new trees planted, so always take account of this when using the maps and written notes. Every effort has been made to make the guide as accurate as possible. The author would be pleased to hear about any changes you may find.

GATES: Although the general advice of the country code is to shut all gates the best advice is to leave the gate as you find it as a gate may have been left open for a particular reason. Only if there is a danger of livestock straying, i.e. into a field of crops or onto a road, should you consider closing an open gate. considered common sense is the pass-word! When you cannot open a gate and have to climb over, please do so at the hinge end where the gate is strongest.

DOGS - *always* keep dogs on a lead, especially on farm land or when near livestock. Never allow your dog to chase sheep.

THE COUNTRY CODE - always follow the country code, in particular **LEAVE NO LITTER,** help protect trees, wild life and plants, and do not light fires at any time.

THE WALKS - for expedience, all walks in the Church Stretton area are described as starting from the Central Avenue Car Park which is also close to the Railway Station. The walks are graded in level of difficulty from one to five. Each walk starts with a brief description, advice on footwear and the state of the paths one can expect.

PUBLIC RIGHTS OF WAY - are footpaths and bridleways protected by law. To me there is nothing more upsetting, on a quiet walk, than confrontation with a landowner because a guide or map includes tracks to which the public do not have access. For this reason I have ensured that all my walks keep strictly to public rights of way. Most footpaths are now signposted and many are also waymarked. Waymarks are in two colours, yellow for footpaths to which only pedestrians have access, and blue for bridleways to which walkers, horses and bicycles have access. The Longmynd is owned by the National trust and all walks use either public footpaths , bridleways, or ancient tracks.

LONE PINE CONNECTIONS: Unlike most other books for children, Malcolm Saville set his books in real places and it was his vivid descriptions of the Shropshire Hills which brought me to Shropshire in 1957. Based at a cottage at the south end of the Long Mynd, Malcolm Saville used many real places in south Shropshire as settings for his stories and I have mentioned, where appropriate, which books go with each walk, and I hope this will add a little interest to the walk for young and old alike who treasure the Lone Pine books, or encourage those to whom these books are unknown to start reading them.

INDEX

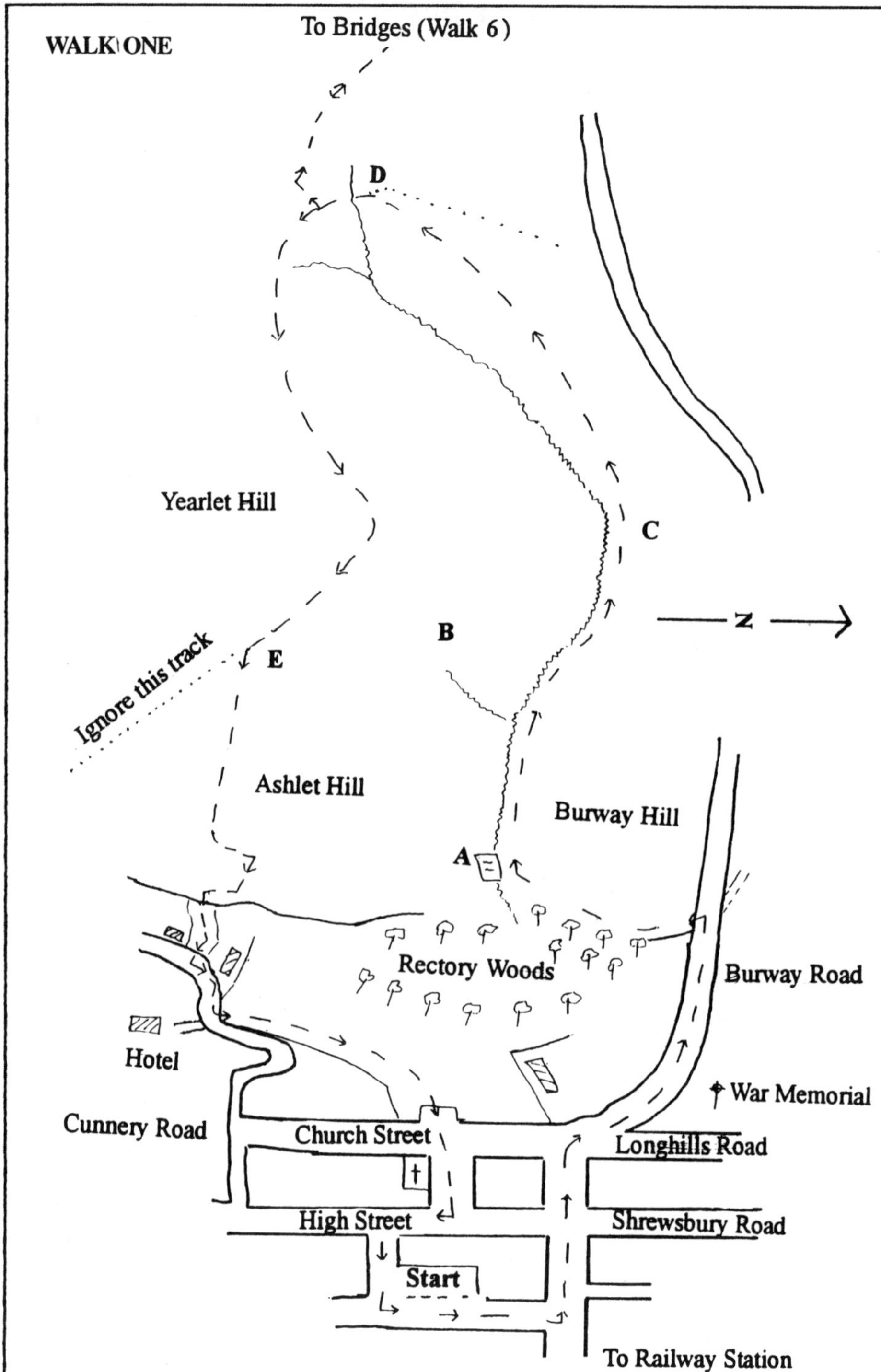
WALK ONE
To Bridges (Walk 6)
D
Yearlet Hill
C
N
B
E
Ignore this track
Ashlet Hill
Burway Hill
A
Rectory Woods
Burway Road
Hotel
War Memorial
Cunnery Road
Church Street
Longhills Road
High Street
Shrewsbury Road
Start
To Railway Station

WALK ONE TOWNBROOK HOLLOW 3½ miles

Townbrook Hollow is so called as the brook once ran (and still does in pipes under the street) down the shop side of Sandford Avenue before it was developed, thus is gets its name the "towns brook".

START: Central Avenue (Pay and Display) Car Park.

GRADE: Two. Good walking under foot with an easy graded rise on the way out and a grassy slope on the return which could be slippery if wet. Good walking shoes are adequate.

REFRESHMENTS: none on the walk, cafés and pubs in the town.

DESCRIPTION: A gentle introduction to the Shropshire Hills, encompassing a quiet attractive valley and a slice of the moorland on top. Following the stream, at first, the walk gently rises to the head of the valley and the edge of the heather moorland. The return affords fine views.

LONE PINE CONNECTIONS: In the last Lone Pine book, Malcolm Saville relocated this valley to a point south of "Witchend" and called it Harkaway Hollow. The water eruption which figures in the story actually took place in Townbrook Hollow in July 1970.

THE WALK: Leave the car park, with the supermarket to your right,and turn left into Central Avenue, then left again into Sandford Avenue. Go over the cross roads by Lloyds Bank and follow Burway Road as far as the cattle grid. Turn left passing the Rectory Woods (open to the public) and bear right at the Reservoir (**A**) into the valley and follow the stream.

At the first side valley (**B**) look up to your left and see the large hole gashed out of the hillside by an underground explosion of water during a thunderstorm in July 1970. Although some 30 years ago it is only now beginning to reseed. The bog there was being fed by rainwater channelled into it from underground sources higher up the hill and at such a rate that the bog was unable to accommodate the water and it simply exploded. Soil strewn right down into the main valley was visible for years afterwards. This part of the valley is a favourite haunt of some of our earliest migrant birds, the Wheatear, small grey bird with white rump, and the Ring Ouzel, rather like a blackbird with a white "clerical type" collar under its chin.

Pass the scree at (**C**), formed by pieces of rock broken away by centuries of weathering from the "Devil's Mouth" the outcrop of rock above you to your right, and follow the track which now starts to climb away from the stream.

At the head of the valley (**D**) another path joins from your right, this goes back to the road, you can probably see some cars, and can be used as an easy return route if you wish. Bear left around the valley head to a grassy patch. Here turn right, leaving Townbrook Hollow and cross over the high ground to see Ashes Hollow. A wider grassy area is now found with "cart tracks" indented in the ground. As a detour, turn right and follow these tracks. Where the tracks fork go right and you soon join more recently made deep rutted tracks. There is a rock tipped hillock ahead. Stop. (**Walkers for "Bridges", turn now to Walk 6**) Here until the early 20th century were "The Guns", a gun emplacement for an artillery range used by the Shropshire and South Staffordshire Yeomanry. The targets were on "Round Hill" away to the south on the other side of Ashes Hollow. If you look carefully, and in the right place, you can still see the level grassy squares where the guns were located. Now retrace your steps to the top of Townbrook Hollow and turn right on regaining the path.

The path still rises until rounding the corner you get a superb view northwards across the Shropshire Plain. The volcano shaped hill is "The Wrekin" and nearer home are Lawley and Caradoc.

You are now on a fairly level path which stretches away before you. Do not, however, follow it as far as you can now see it. Continue ahead until you have passed the side valley (**B**) on your left. Take the first path left at (**E**) , a narrower path which gives from a small triangular grassy patch and takes you along the side of the valley. The Devil's Mouth should be to your immediate left on the far side of Townbrook. On breasting the ridge ahead you have a marvellous view of the Stretton Vale and will see the grassy path dropping away downhill towards the town. At the bottom of the grassy slope, bear right to the edge of the woods and then turn right for a short distance on a "level path" to find the "Hundred Steps" which take you down to Cunnery Road. Turn left. Just round the corner turn left again into "Rectory Fields" and drop down passing the Rectory Woods again with the Parish Church ahead. To return to the start, pass the Church towards the shops and turn right then left into the car park.

With Callow Hollow, Ashes is the most exciting of the Longmynd Valleys, even on the busiest days the upper reaches are always quiet. You can make a circular walk from Little Stretton or Church Stretton. From Church Stretton leave by Ludlow Road and join the walk at the Ragleth Inn. There is also a bus service.

START: Ragleth Inn, Little Stretton.

GRADE: Three. Moderate. If you take your time its a good days walk. Paths well defined and in good condition, isolated boggy or muddy patches.

DESCRIPTION: A delightful valley of marked contrasts. Wide and flat at first it narrows in the mid stretch where erosion has so worn away the stream side path that a path on a higher level is now necessary. Farther up, the valley widens again in a gentler less rugged stretch. The path then steepens before emerging on to the heather covered moor of the Longmynd . The return is along a wide easy track affording fine views.

REFRESHMENTS: Two very good Inn's in Little Stretton, the Ragleth Inn (**A**) and the Green Dragon, (**B**) both do excellent meals at reasonable prices.

ALTERNATIVE WALKS: (1) turn right at "G" and walk up this side valley, over the brow and down into Townbrook Hollow to return via Walk one in reverse to Church Stretton. (2) Take the side valley at "H" to "Pole Cottage" at "J".(3) From "Boiling Well "I" return to Church Stretton following the road.

PARKING: limited space by the stream at (**C**) or in the lay-by on the A49 at (**D**).

LONE PINE CONNECTIONS: Ashes is typical of the countryside Malcolm Saville had in mind when describing the area in general and could perhaps pass for "Dark Hollow" and "Hatchholt", characteristics for both valleys are present here. This valley was a particular favourite of the Saville family. Pole Bank is described in "Mystery at Witchend" as being marked by "a cairn of stones" now replaced by a Topograph. When that book was written in 1943 the metalled road did not exist and would have been no more than a rough track similar, perhaps, to that which now traverses Pole Bank. Pole Cottage was the inspiration for "Beacon Cottage" in "The Neglected Mountain", "Strangers at Witchend"and as "Wildmoor Cottage" in "Wings over Witchend" although it was, in that book, moved south of the Gliding Club. On the return leg you will see the Gliding Station and the state forest which feature in "Wings over Witchend".

THE WALK. Go up the lane past "The Ragleth" (**A**) and turn right. Cross the stream and stile and walk through two fields until on passing the "National Trust" sign cross the footbridge and turn left.

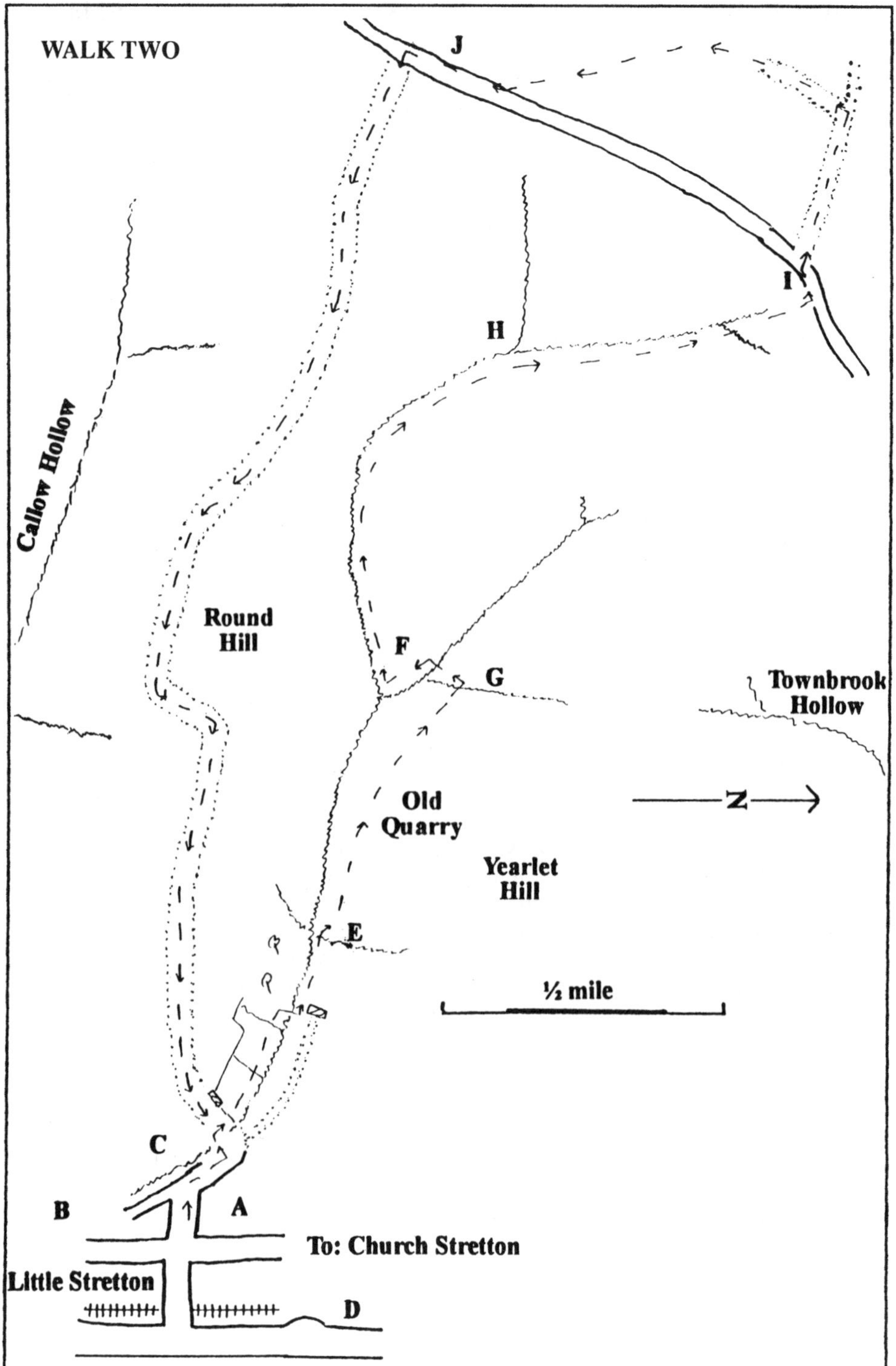
WALK TWO
J
Callow Hollow
H
I
Round
Hill
F
G
Townbrook
Hollow
Old
Quarry
N
Yearlet
Hill
E
½ mile
C
B
A
To: Church Stretton
Little Stretton
D

The valley bottom is wide and flat here and the track still bears the faint indentations made by the wheels of the carts going to and from the old quarry. The track, however, has been seriously eroded over the years by the stream which now leaves scarcely enough room for a footpath. Cross the side valley at (**E**) but go no farther on the wide track by the stream as this has been completely washed away round the bend ahead. Take the narrow path which climbs gently up the valley side, this soon levels off and after passing the quarry you have a fine view of the valley ahead. The valley divides at (**F**) and from the viewpoint you can see both valleys. Your route is up the valley to the left of the fork and from this angle you have a bird's eye view of the the next stretch.. This "diversion" is a blessing in disguise for it has some lovely views.

Another stream crosses your path at (**G**). Cross this stream and turn first left. From the high ground you can see a grassy path a little way up the other side of the new valley. Drop down to cross the main stream and go up the grassy slope to the path and turn left, passing a Hawthorn Tree and rounding the "bluff" the path widens as it comes back again into the main valley above the fork.

From here a different valley unfolds, wider and gentler than the first section, with several pleasant paths. The rich heather clad hills on your left and grassy hills on your right are the haunt of Wheatears, Cuckoos, Stonechats, Whinchats and Ring Ouzels. Continue ahead up the main valley until you reach the road at "Boiling Well". (**I**) Turn left.

"The Boiling Well" is so called on account of the water bubbling up from the underground spring; alas, years of pollution caused by gravels being washed down from the nearby track have filled it in. Walk up that track to the ridge and turn left along a wide dirt track to the summit where there is a Topograph and an O.S. triangulation point. Ahead of you you will see some trees, walk down to them. This was where "Pole Cottage" used to be (**J**). Used as an RAF Falconry Station during the War it had various uses over the years until vandals reduced it to dereliction and the National Trust were forced to demolish it.

You will find Meadow Pipits galore up here, the most common of the little birds, but the favourite for most people is The Curlew whose haunting cry is sure to be heard, a large bird with a long curved beak.

Now walk south along the road until you come to a wide grassy track on your left marked with a signpost "Little Stretton". Away to the south is the Gliding Station and ahead the track skirts round "Round Hill" where the targets for "the Guns" were situated.(see walk one). Further south the long flat outline of the Black Mountains is usually visible while to the south-east the humpy Malvern Hills can be seen. Turn left at the post along the track and follow it back to the start.

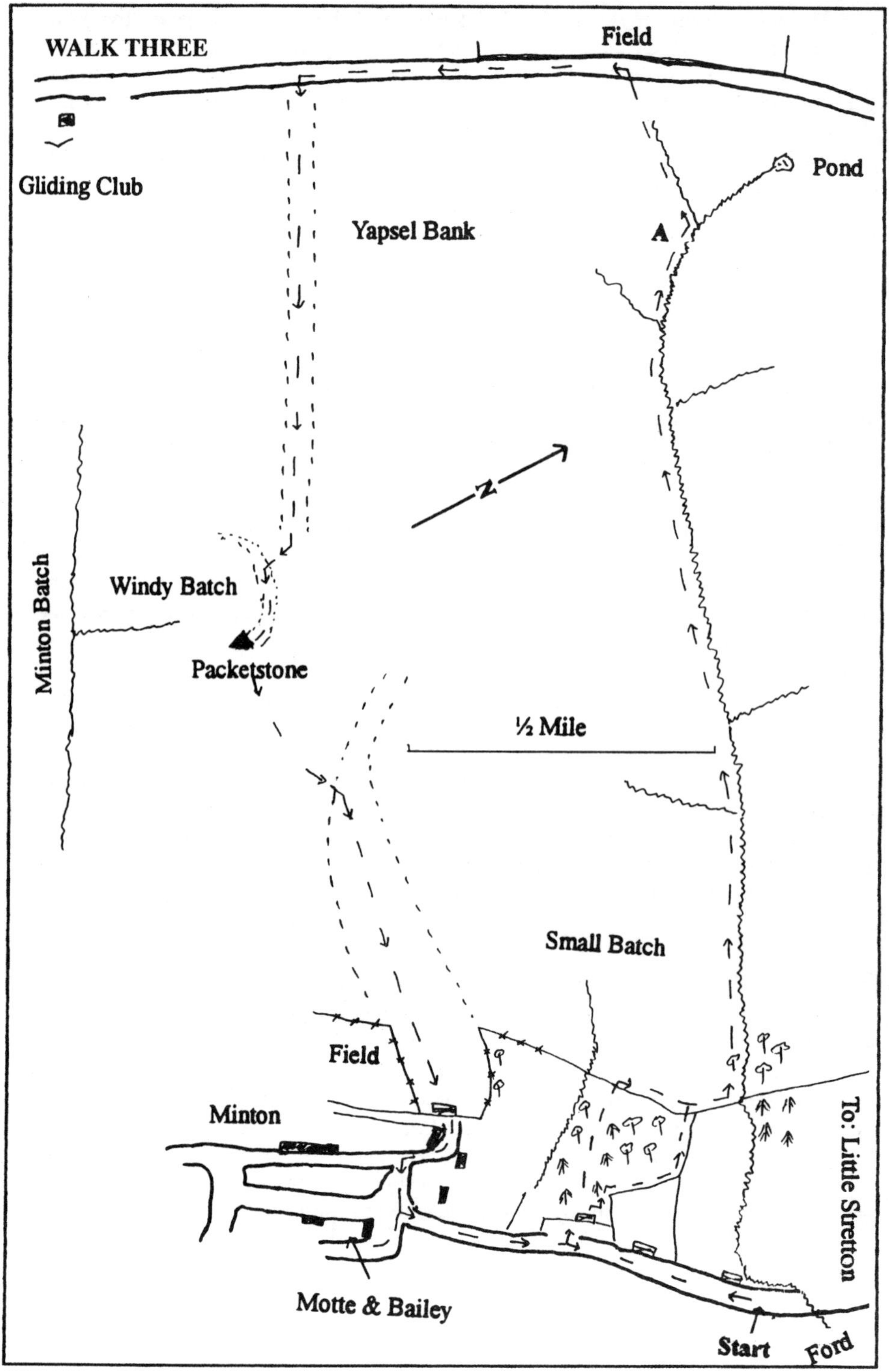
WALK THREE
Field
Gliding Club
Pond
Yapsel Bank
A
N
Minton Batch
Windy Batch
Packetstone
½ Mile
Small Batch
Field
Minton
To: Little Stretton
Motte & Bailey
Start
Ford

WALK THREE CALLOW HOLLOW 4½ miles

Callow Hollow is the longest and wildest of all the Longmynd Valleys. Always quiet and secluded on account its unobtrusiveness it brings great rewards for those taking the trouble to seek it out. With its scattering of trees it is alive with birds all the year round.

START: From the lane between Little Stretton and the hamlet of Minton . From Church Stretton go to Little Stretton and turn right by The Ragleth Inn, then turn left at the stream and just ahead fork right. After a mile cross the stream and park on the right where the lane widens.

GRADE: three. On well defined paths throughout, the going is a little steeper than walks 1 and 2 in the upper reaches of the valley. Paths usually dry but the isolated boggy patch is only to be expected. Crossing the stream is also involved.

DESCRIPTION: the difficulty of access coupled with its remoteness from any significant population makes Callow the least frequented of any valley, yet it is one of most fascinating. The steep slopes on its northern side at the start contrast with the gentle slopes on the south side which abound with a multitude of paths. The return leg follows an ancient pack horse road.

REFRESHMENTS: The Ragleth Inn and The Green Dragon Inn, at Little Stretton.

PARKING: Park on the right after the stream where the lane widens.

LONE PINE CONNECTIONS: In "The Man with Three Fingers" Malcolm Saville has an episode which takes place in "Callow Batch" and the swimming pool he describes in which the twins went for a bathe does exist here in Callow Hollow. In that story, however, Callow has been moved to a position south of "Witchend" but there is no doubting the inspiration for Callow Batch as the description of it in the story is exactly as it actually is.

THE WALK: From the car walk on towards Minton village passing two field gates. At a small conifer plantation marked with the National Trust Sign "Longmynd - Wynd Hill" turn right. A level footpath follows the fence on the right bordering the fields, but this may get difficult in high summer with high ferns and vicious stinging nettles in which case follow the wider clear track straight ahead. This emerges into Smallbatch Valley where you turn right. At the top of the slope is a stupendous view right up the valley, which, if you follow the lower path,you don't see. Continue now down into the valley, but beware of the loose stones. At the stream turn left and follow the stream right up to the end of the valley.

You can see now the steep slopes on your right, yet on your left the valley is opened right back with many paths on the higher slopes. There are several paths in this section of the valley near the stream, take whichever you choose, you won't get lost as the valley narrows later and all paths eventually meet by the stream. At the top where the high valley sides give way to the flatter moor, (**A**) fork left where the streams divide and head towards the skyline where there is a lone tree. At first you won't see the road but you will see the fence beyond or a vehicle passing along it. At the road turn left. You are now walking along the Portway, a track from the ancient Briton era now, alas, here, tarmaced, but there are stretches to the north in original condition.

On the brow of the next ridge, and in sight of the Gliding Club, turn left onto a wide dirt track which can clearly be seen ahead as it climbs over Yapsel Bank. This is another very ancient track and eventually narrows into a footpath which skirts "Windy Batch" heading for a rocky outcrop. This is the "Packetstone" a hump of rock which gets its name from the days of pack horses using the track. Here, before descending into the valley, the drover would stand on the rock to adjust the load on the pony's back. Continue down hill now following a well defined path which later joins another wider track and continues downhill into Minton. More signs of the old road with deep indentations in the ground will be seen. At the village green turn left then left again, signposted "Little Stretton" your car is at the bottom of the hill.

WALK FOUR BATCH VALLEY 6 miles

Batch Valley is one of the longest valleys on the Longmynd. Batch is a local name for "valley" as in Minton Batch for example.

START: Central Avenue Car Park, or you can go by bus to "The Yew Tree Inn" All Stretton to start from there.

GRADE: Two. Good walking on dry paths, apart from the odd boggy patch in the upper reaches of the valley.

REFRESHMENTS: The Yew Tree Inn, All Stretton.

DESCRIPTION: The walk from Church Stretton to All Stretton is worth doing as there are some surprisingly good views. Batch valley begins on a metalled road which soon ends and for a little further is a rough track; once beyond the last house the valley narrows and steepens. The walk then crosses an attractive part of the moor giving superb views from the high ground over Haddon Hill.

LONE PINE CONNECTIONS: The reservoir, seen on the return leg, was the inspiration for "Hatcholt" in "Mystery at Witchend" and subsequent books.

THE WALK: Leave the car park and turn left, then left again into Sandford Avenue. Cross the road by Lloyds Bank and turn right along Shrewsbury Road. At (**A**) turn left into Cardingmill Valley and at (**B**) turn right into Madeira Walk. Emerging from the trees onto a rough track at (**C**) turn left and crossing the cattle grid turn right up a short steep hill. *(For an easier level walk from (C) cross the track and take footpath (D),see walk 9 for details).*

Take the most noticeable of the various tracks at the top. (**E**) is an exceptionally good view point looking down onto All Stretton and the Shropshire Plain. The distant hill is The Wrekin, and nearer are Lawley and across to your right Caradoc. Continue ahead along the path which eventually passes a cottage where it turns left and brings you down into Batch Valley by a grassy slope, crossing the stream by a concrete bridge turn left. *(For the village and Inn, turn right).*

Now follow the rough track up the valley for half a mile, it then cross the stream by a ford and becomes grassy. After passing the last holiday home the valley narrows. Keep on the path with the stream to your left as it zig-zags up the valley, narrowing in the upper reaches and boggy in places.

WALK FOUR

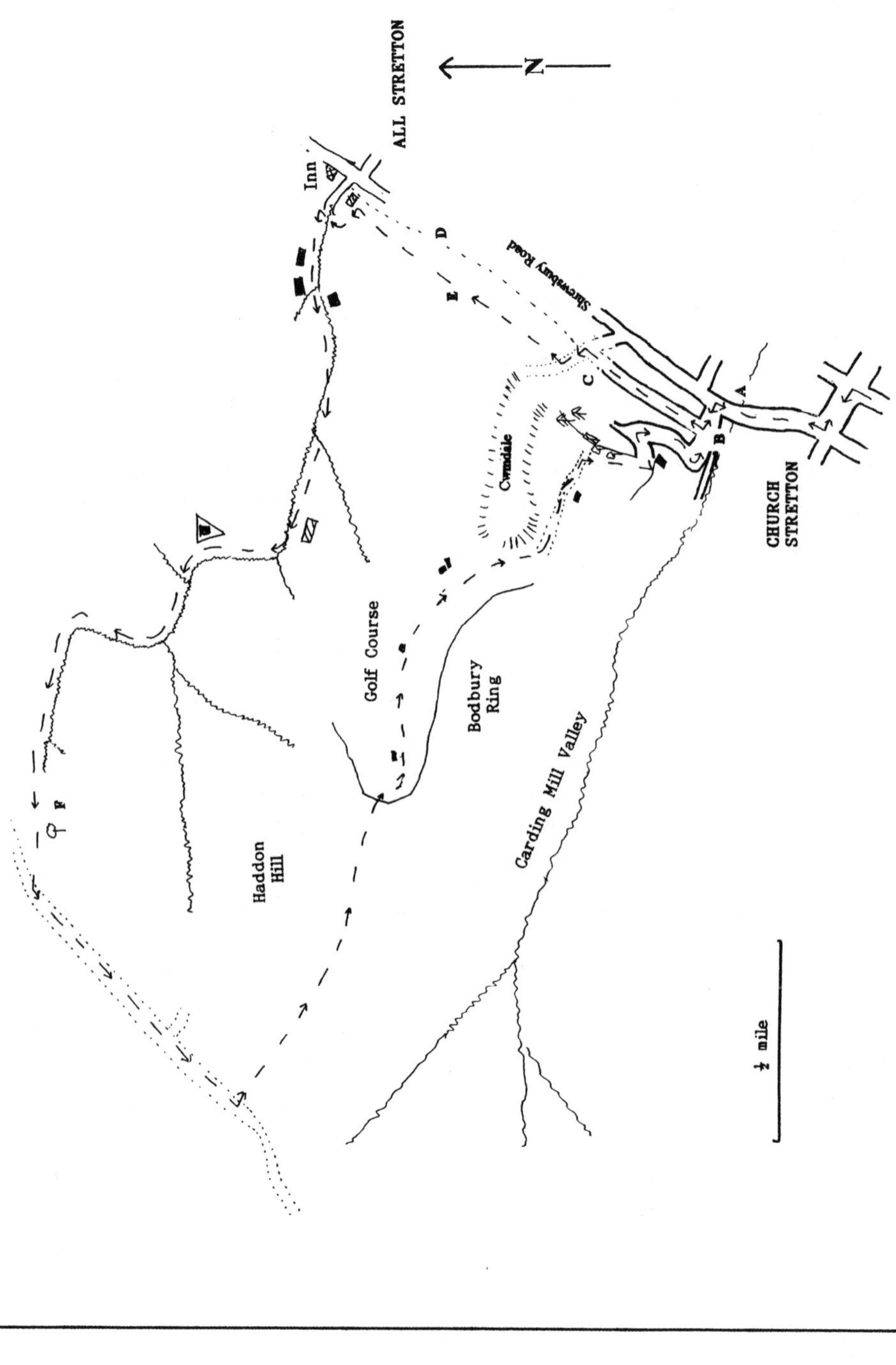
ALL STRETTON
N
Inn
D
E
Shrewsbury Road
C
A
B
CHURCH STRETTON
Cwmdale
Golf Course
Bodbury Ring
Carding Mill Valley
Haddon Hill
F
½ mile

Emerging from the valley at (**F**) pass a solitary shrivelled-up hawthorn tree close by the track on your right and head towards the skyline. Now you are on the moor and straight ahead can see a large solitary tree. Passing near to the tree you will see on your right a field fence. On reaching a wide grassy track with a field gate near on your right , turn left.

There is some fine heather here in late summer when Haddon Hill to the left really does look like the "purple headed mountain".

Listen out for the Red Grouse with its distinctive "cuck-cuck" call, a large brown bird which flies low over the heather, the Lapwing, a medium size black and white bird which in spring has a most amazing flight display and the Ring Ouzel which frequents this part of the moor and in summer can often be seen singing from its perch on top of the heather.

Walk along the wide track passing a cairn of stones which marks a footpath traversing the north side of Haddon; because the track is not easy to describe I suggest you continue until the next track, a wide grassy track which traverses the southern side of the Hill. Now turn left along this track. Below you to your right is Carding Mill Valley while from the top of the second rise an excellent view of Bodbury Ring can be enjoyed. When the wide track ends bear slightly left on a narrower grassy path which drops down through a series of indistinct paths between the heather until the Golf Course comes into view. To your right you can now see the Cardingmill Valley reservoir.

By the 10th green go through the wicket gate bearing right to join a path well marked by public footpath waymark posts sporting the yellow arrow. Pass a brown hut then near the black hut with "13th Tee" painted on the door, two paths diverge, keep straight on, don't go left. A brown hut and a black hut are then passed before you skirt around "Cwmdale". On passing a 5th hut near a ship's bell, descend the slope and at a gate with a blue post turn right keeping on the hill side of the line of trees until you come to the Golf Club. Now turn left through the little gate and join the road which takes you back to the start.

WALK FIVE

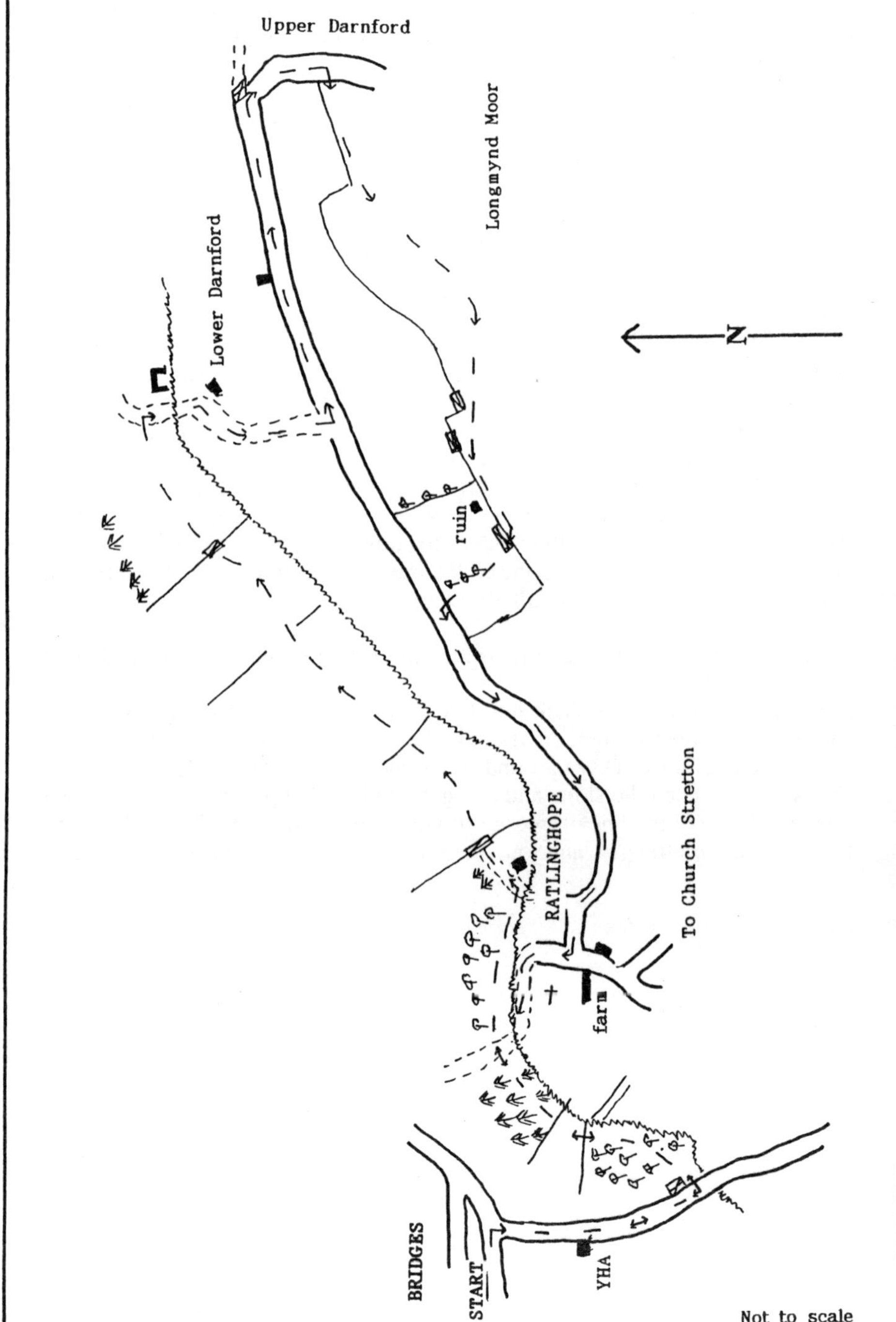

Upper Darnford
Longmynd Moor
Lower Darnford
N
ruin
RATLINGHOPE
To Church Stretton
farm
BRIDGES
START
YHA
Not to scale

A unique valley for the Shropshire Hills not being part of the Longmynd proper yet attached to it. The valley is on the western side of the Mynd. Ratlinghope Church's claim to fame, is the starting point for Rev.Donald Carr's fateful and almost fatal "Walk in the Snow" when he nearly lost his life in a blizzard, and also that it once used a heating boiler obtained from Windsor Castle.

START: Bridges Inn, near Ratlinghope.

LONE PINE CONNECTIONS: The Bridges Inn is the "Hope Anchor Inn" in "Seven White Gates" and "Negelected Mountain"

GRADE: two. Easy walking on well defined paths, an isolated boggy patch on the way out but nothing to worry about, good walking shoes or boots advisable.

DESCRIPTION: A most agreeable valley, varied scenery with trees in the lower parts, fields and then the heather and bracken of the Longmynd plateau. The outward path uses part of "The Shropshire Way"

REFRESHMENTS: The Horseshoes Inn does bar lunches.

HOW TO GET THERE: From Church Stretton take the "Burway Road" and fork right on the top of the hill. At the foot of the hill the other side, turn left signposted "Bishop's Castle" then turn next right , signposted "Bridges".

PARKING: opposite the Horseshoes Inn,Bridges.

THE WALK: From the Inn walk back past the Youth Hostel to the stone bridge turn left over waymarked stile into woods with the stream to your right.. The waymarks on the outward stretch are either a yellow arrow or a white buzzard on a black background, the sign of "The Shropshire Way". Walk through the woods and just before bridge bear left to a waymarked stile and cross field beyond. Follow narrow path through pine wood. On emerging from woods cross track to waymarked stile and continue ahead near stream. Go ahead over two more waymarked stiles and then turn left opposite red-brick cottage near the stream into an open valley. The track up the valley is easy to follow, most gates and stiles being waymarked.

Above Lower Darnford turn right and follow track past house to the lane where turn left. Follow lane as far as the National Trust sign. Cross cattle grid and turn right. The path and the hedge(on right) soon part company (see map) but keep straight ahead on a sheep track and they will eventually rejoin.

At a wide grassy area the fence again turns right and you will see a farm gate but ignore it and still continue ahead dropping down into a marshy gully and up the other side.

Just pass the ruin of Marsh Farm pass a gate and cross the stile beyond it. Go downhill towards a row of trees just beyond which is a gate into the lane. Turn left. On reaching Ratlinghope Church turn right and follow the track as far as the pine wood. Turn left over stile and retrace your outward path back to the start.

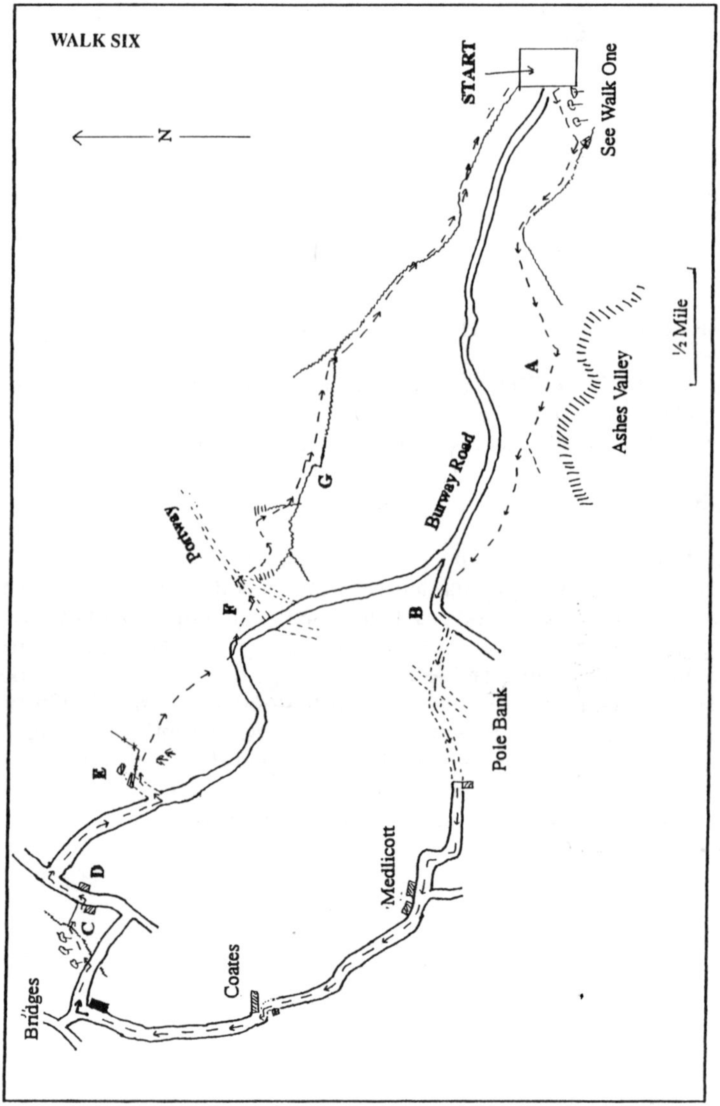

WALK SIX BRIDGES & CARDINGMILL VALLEY 10 Miles

A lovely walk with a meal halfway is the object of this walk. If you want to get to the Inn for lunch start the walk no later than 10 o'clock.

START: Central Avenue (Pay & Display) Car Park.

GRADE: Five (on account of the length)

DESCRIPTION: This is a delightful walk, starting in the attractive Townbrook Valley it crosses the Longmynd Moor into the lush green Onny Valley. Some boggy patches. Boots or good walking shoes essential.

REFRESHMENTS: The Horseshoes Inn, Bridges

ADJUSTMENTS: (1) if you find this walk too long drive as far as the Boiling Well (**B**) and make a circular walk of it from there, this will reduce the distance by 4 miles, or (2) walk the whole walk to Bridges and take a taxi back.

LONE PINE CONNECTIONS: The "Bridges Inn" features in "Seven White Gates" and "The Neglected Mountain" as "Hope Anchor Inn". The Lightspout waterfall and valley became "Dark Hollow" in several stories.

THE WALK: Follow instructions in walk one up Townbrook Hollow as far as (**A**) "The Guns"; here, where it says "Stop" continue ahead following the well worn track which skirts around Ashes Hollow. When the track turns grassy fork right and head for the ridge from which the track crossing Pole Bank is clearly visible.

On reaching the road turn left and at (**B**) take the wide rough track which crosses Pole Bank. It then descends into the Onny Valley beyond which rises "The Stiperstones" crowned by the "Devil's Chair". The remote cottage by the field gate is the location for "Appledore" in "Mystery at Witchend".

Join the road at the foot of the hill and turn right past Medlicott Farm . At Coates, the next farm, turn left then right around the farmhouse and crossing a cattle grid regain the lane. The white building ahead is not the Inn but is only a ten minute walk from it.

The return walk starts from the Inn; turn right at the road junction and pass the Youth Hostel. Just before the stone walled bridge turn left over a stile marked with the Shropshire Way sign and walk through the woods. At (**C**) turn right over another low bridge eventually rejoining the lane opposite Ratlinghope Manor (**D**). Turn left. At the next road junction turn right as signposted Church Stretton and walk as far as the cattle grid. By the National Trust sign turn left for Belmore Cottage.(**E**) Fork right here onto a grassy track. Just beyond the bend in the road fork left onto a new grassy track.

(**If you left your car at the Boiling Well (B) continue along the road to your starting point**). At (**F**) turn left along a new wider track. Walk as far as two sets of posts driven into the ground and go the second set of which one is painted white. Cross "The Portway" and take the wide grassy path heading east, with a bog in the hollow to your right. Your grassy track bends left and then turns right down a side valley. At the bottom cross the bog and follow a well defined path with the stream on your right. At the "Lightspout Waterfall" (**G**) descent is difficult and needs care. The waterfall was featured in "Mystery at Witchend" Follow the stream to Cardingmill Valley and turn right for Church Stretton.

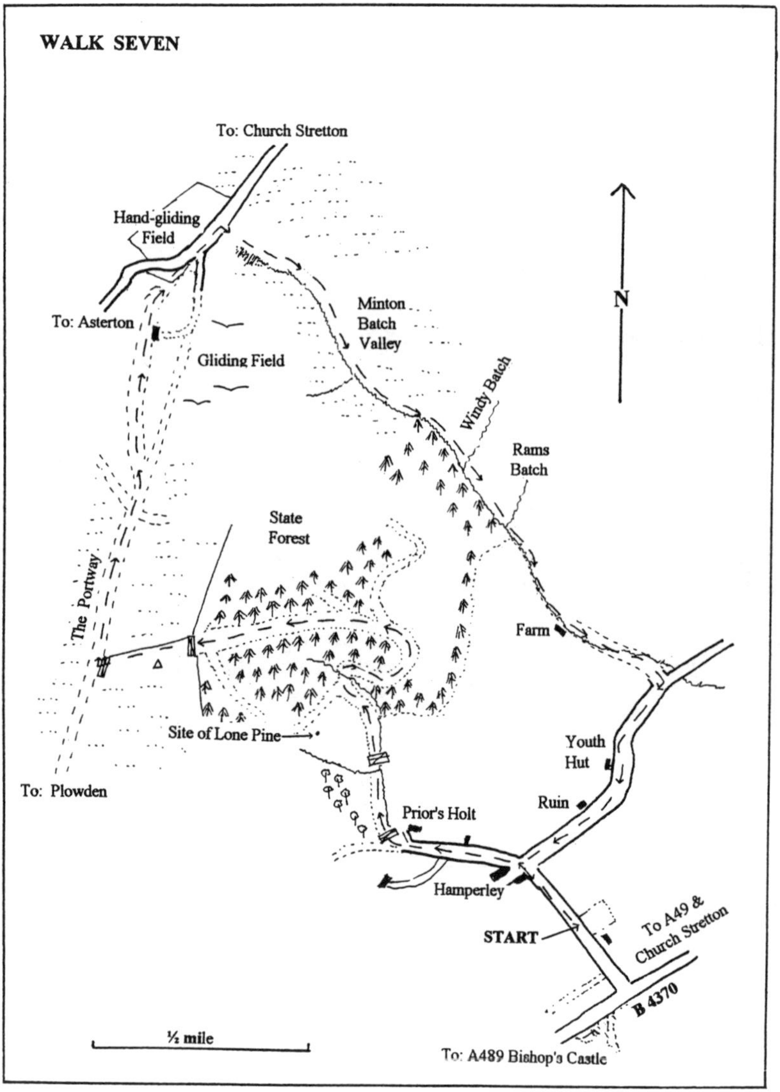

WALK SEVEN NUT BATCH & MINTON BATCH 5 miles

This walk is the most southerly on the Long Mynd and gives some superb views, you also have a chance of watching the activities at the Gliding Station.

START: From the lane approaching Hamperley

GRADE: Two. Easy walking on well defined tracks. Good shoes adequate.

REFRESHMENTS: none on the walk. The Railway Inn at Marshbook(or Onnybrook as it is called in the books), does bar meals.

HOW TO GET THERE: From Church Stretton drive south on the A49 for two miles until you turn right onto the B4370 signposted "Bishop's Castle". Two miles further, at the brow of a long hill which rises from the railway crossing, turn first right as signposted "Hamperley/Prior's Holt".

PARKING: Wide verge on the right near the camping field above Hamperley.

LONE PINE CONNECTIONS: This is the very heart of the Lone Pine country, everything that happens in 15 of the 20 Lone Pine Books has some connection with, or occurs in, this area.

THE WALK: With your back to the car walk ahead down the hill. At the foot of the hill, at the cross roads is;on your left, "Ingles Farm"(Hamperley). Continue ahead as signposted "Prior's Holt". The last house on the right is the Lone Piners home "Witchend". Continue ahead on the rough track, which is a bridleway, a forestry commission track. Above to your left is what remains of the "Larch Wood" most of which has been cut down but some Larches still remain higher up the hillside.

The track passes through a second gate by which is a sign "Forestry Commission - Long Mynd". The forest played the central roll in the book "Wings over Witchend" in which thieves stole the young trees for the Christmas trade. After a wide swing to the right the track still climbs and just beyond a waymark post you will come to a fork of tracks, the track to the right swings away around the edge of Minton Batch valley but use the other track, this goes more or less straight on. Continue ahead on this track until you see a field gate ahead. Go through the gate and continue ahead by the perimeter fence of the gliding field passing the notice "To the Portway". Shortly, on your left, you will see an Ordnance Survey Triangulation post which is the site of "Peter's Rock" in the book "Strangers at Witchend". From this point look north, can you see, beneath the highest crest, a row of trees? These surround the area where stood (Pole Cottage) which featured in "Wings over Witchend" and also as "Beacon Cottage" in "Strangers at Witchend".

On reaching the Portway turn right and head for the gliding club. Pass a wooden signpost and ahead bear left along "The Scenic Route" a wide grassy path well marked by white posts. There are a few seats to give you time for rest and admire the view. On passing the "windsock" go straight ahead, the next set of white posts is not immediately visible but soon come into view and then follow the path, slightly forking right, to a stile and thence to the road. Turn right.

Pass the National Trust sign. There is a fence on the left of the road. When the fence ends turn right, off the road, and head down into the valley with the Gliding field to your right. *Keep to the left of the bog* and later to the left of the stream and the path is self-evident. On reaching a "T" junction where the farm track meets the lane, turn right and at Hamperley turn left to return to the start.

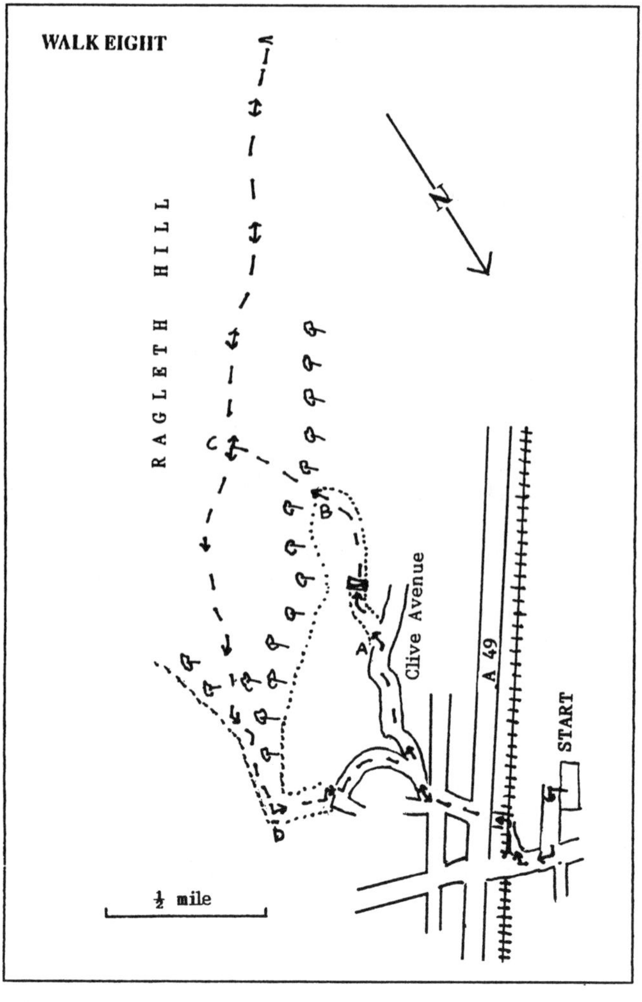

WALK EIGHT **RAGLETH HILL** **3 miles**

Ragleth is the most southerly of the hills flanking the east side of the Stretton vale and this short walk can be accomplished quite comfortably in a half day.

START: Central Avenue(pay and display) Car Park.

GRADE: Four. Although a short walk there is a stiff climb and descent on grassy slopes,slippery if wet but not dangerous. Requires some energy!

DESCRIPTION: Ragleth is a short and narrow hill; the views from the ridge path are quite unique in this area being entirely uninterrupted in almost every direction.

REFRESHMENTS: none.

THE WALK: Leave the car park and turn left then right into Sandford Avenue. Go down to the Railway Station and cross the line by the footbridge and then cross the A49 road. Fork right by the Sandford Nursing Home up the hill of Clive Avenue. Fork right again by "Holmwood" still climbing Clive Avenue.

At (**A**)pass the bungalow "Avenhills" and fork left up a grassy track alongside a wooden fence. The track peters out in a field but continue in the same direction towards the trees where you will find a stile. Many years ago I watched as a Barn Owl "worked" this field one early August evening.

Go over waymarked stile (**B**) and follow the track straight uphill through the trees emerging onto the hillside. Now it's a case of making your way to the top by the most suitable way possible, but it is, none-the-less quite a climb so stop and look back at the ever widening view.

On reaching the ridge path, (**C**) turn right and make your way to the end of the hill. From the pole which marks the summit there is a superb view. To the south you can see the road and railway wending their way to Craven Arms and Ludlow. To the west you almost have a bird's eye view of the Longmynd and the deep valleys which cut into it from the eastern side. Ashes Valley is the nearest. South of that you can see the state forest which features in the book "Wings Over Witchend", the "Witchend" valley itself is the second valley to the south. Away to the east the humpy outline of the Malvern Hills and on a very clear day, low and flat beyond the Malvern's you can see the western escarpment of the Cotswolds.

Turn back now along the ridge to the northern extremity where the descent is more gradual than the way up. At the bottom , near the fence, (**D**) turn left still continuing down hill. This wood is a carpet of bluebells in April and May. The path crosses a stile to continue steeply down emerging into Ragleth Road by the bungalows. Turn left to return by Clive Avenue to the start.

WALK NINE

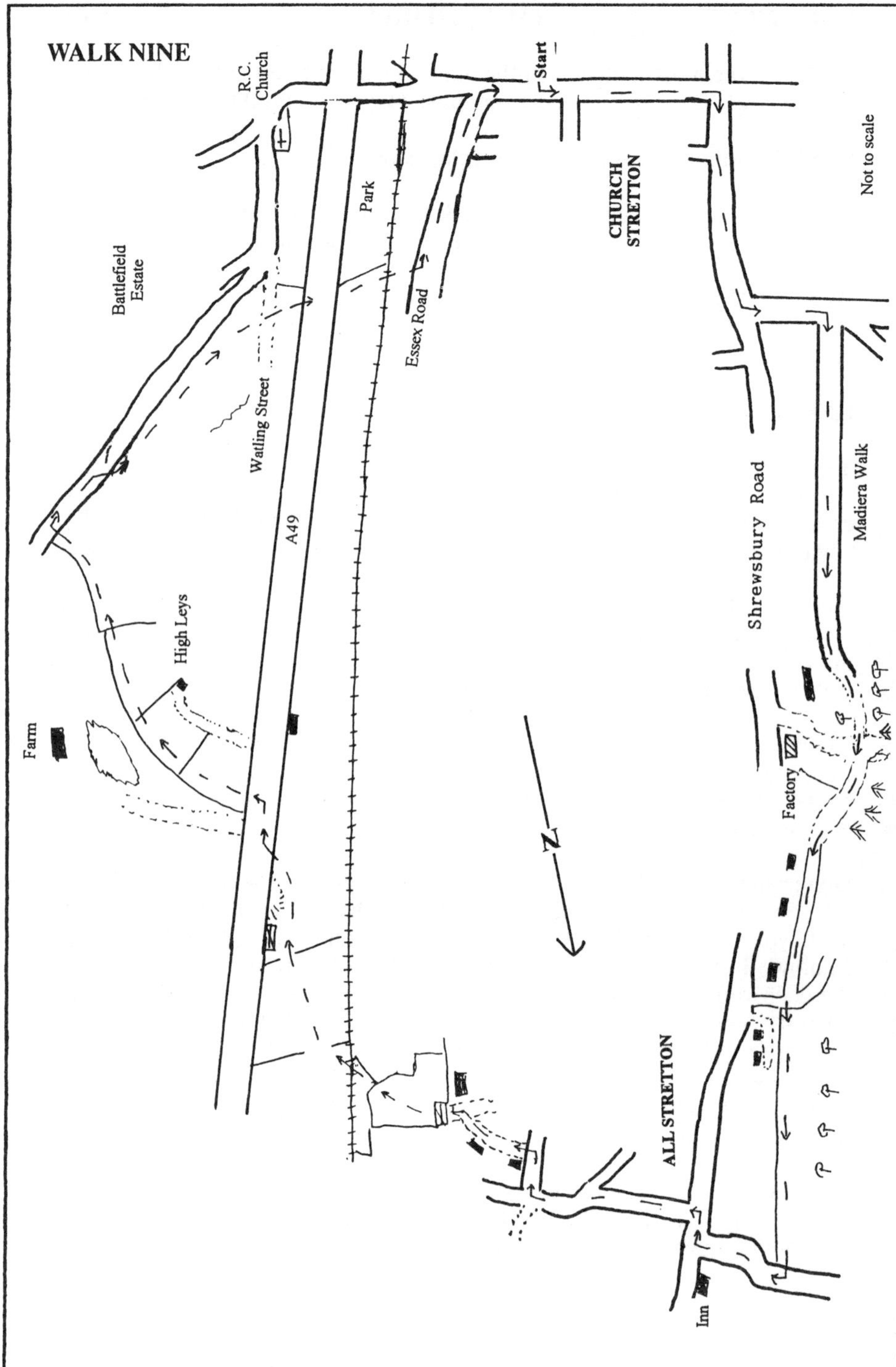
R.C. Church
Start
Battlefield Estate
Park
CHURCH STRETTON
Not to scale
Watling Street
Essex Road
A49
Shrewsbury Road
Madiera Walk
High Leys
Farm
Factory
N
ALL STRETTON
Inn

A pleasant walk in the Stretton Vale linking two of the Strettons, Church Stretton and All Stretton, suitable for an evening.

START: Central Avenue (pay & display) car park.

GRADE: One. A level walk mostly on good paths.

DESCRIPTION: After leaving the houses behind the outward walk gives some fine views. The Yew Tree Inn is nicely situated at the half way point and welcomes children. The return walk is across fields.

REFRESHMENTS: The Yew Tree Inn,All Stretton.

LONE PINE CONNECTIONS: None

THE WALK: From the car park, turn left into Sandford Avenue and at the cross roads by the Banks turn right along Shrewsbury Road. Turn left at the signpost "Cardingmill Valley" and then first right into Madeira Walk.

On emerging from the trees at the end of Madeira Walk cross the rough track and go through the wicket gate nearly opposite. From here follow the path to All Stretton. There is a very good view just after joining this path which then drops down hill before continuing behind houses by a hedged in path. Cross the Tarmac road near a red-brick house and continue ahead through the iron kissing gate. Go straight ahead with houses on your right.

On reaching Batch Valley turn right to All Stretton. In the village turn right. ***(the Yew Tree Inn is just to the left)*** and then turn first left by the letter box. Walk down the lane and shortly after crossing the stream turn right by a second letter box into Heighways Lane. On passing the house called "Westbeech" turn left along a narrow grassy path between houses. Go through field gate and cross field towards far right-hand corner and cross railway. Bear to the right in field through the gap where the gate used to be and cross the next field diagonally, all the time getting closer to the main road . Skirt around crater beyond field gate and find the concealed stile beyond. Cross the road when it is safe to do so.

Just past the farm drive opposite is a stile partially hidden by bushes. Go over stile and continue ahead with the hedge on your left and the track to "High Leys" on your right. In the fourth field you will come to the grassy remains of a very old track which bends to the left to join the lane. Turn right. Just beyond the "30" sign is a stile at the top of a short flight of steps. Cross the field heading for the electricity pylons and then cross "Watling Street" by means of two stiles. This stretch of Watling Street is as near as one can get these days to the actual Roman road for here it is not made up. Re-cross the A49 and the railway as signposted and turn left in Essex Road for the town centre.

WALK TEN

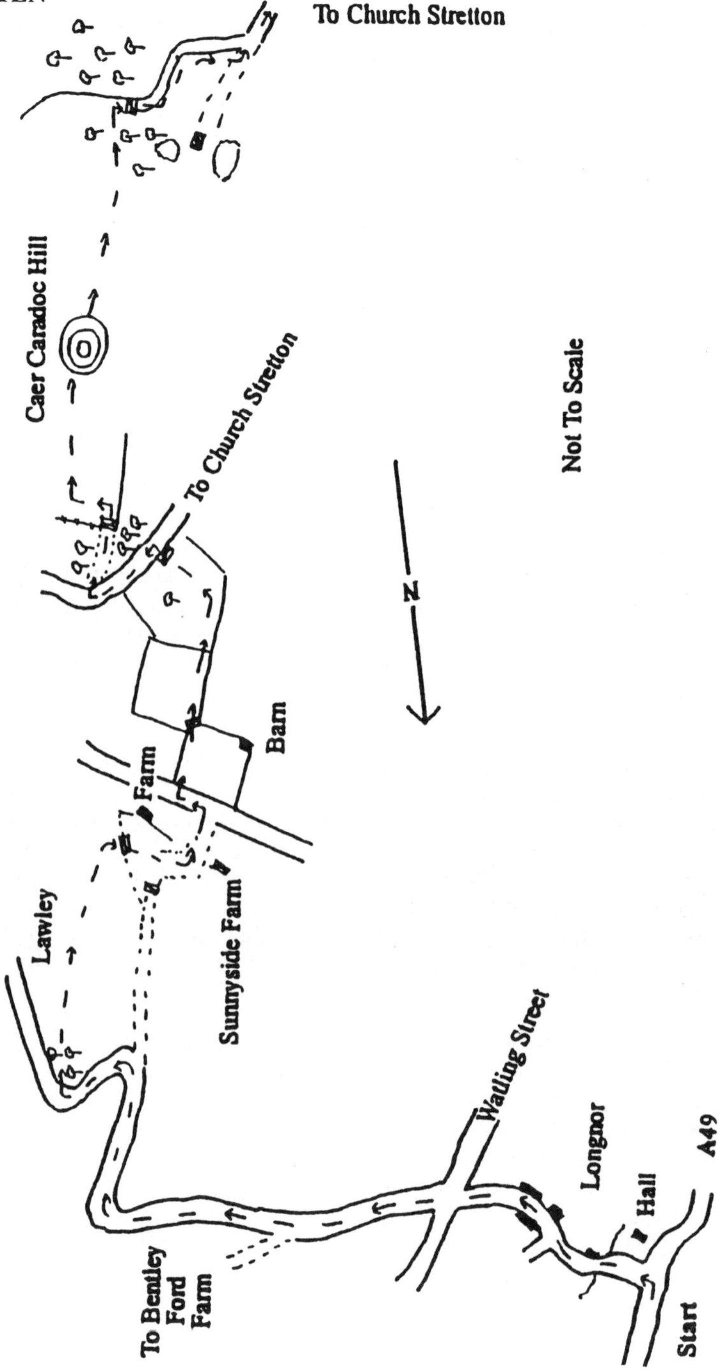

To Church Stretton
Caer Caradoc Hill
To Church Stretton
Not To Scale
N
Barn
Farm
Lawley
Sunnyside Farm
Watling Street
Longnor
Hall
A49
To Bentley Ford Farm
Start

This is linear walk. Go by bus from Church Stretton to Longnor and walk back over the hills (bus once every two hours)

START: Bus stop near Longnor on the A49 north of Church Stretton

GRADE: Three. Two steep slimbs but dry underfoot.

DESCRIPTION: Starting on the lane at Longnor, the walk climbs over Lawley before ascending Caradoc. Extremely goods views throughout.

REFRESHMENTS: none. It's a take-your-own-picnic walk.

THE WALK: From the bus stop on the A49 walk back and turn left as signposted "Longnor", At the end of the village fork right as signposted "Frodesley 2¼". At the cross roads signposted "Lawley 1¼" go straight on. The road crossing from left to right is the original line of the Roman road "Watling Street". At the foot of Lawley the road makes a double bend; the track at the first bend, with a bridleway sign, goes on the level along the west side of Lawley and can be used to avoid the climb, otherwise at the next bend is a "passing come parking space"; leave the road and cross this parking space to a narrow path climbing up the hill to a stile, then through the trees onto the open hillside. The path over the top is now quite clear. There is a small Ancient British camp is on the first hump, and fine views north over Shrewsbury and the Shropshire Plain. The Wrekin is the hill slightly to the north east.

On reaching the south end of Lawley find the track past Sunnyside Farm. Turn left at the lane and then immediately turn right, there is a wicket gate at the top of a short flight of stone steps. Follow path alongside hedge,at first on left, then in 2nd field on right towards Caradoc(a lone tree in middle of 3rd field guides you to gate). At next lane turn left and at top of hill turn sharp right onto a mud track into the woods.

Go through the gate and turn left uphill to pylon post, then turn right and follow crest path to summit. The ancient camp is reputed to be one of the last strongholds of Caractacus before his battle with Ostorius Scapula's legion in A.D.50 the site of which again is reputed to be the new housing estate "Battlefield". The area enclosed by the triple ditches is 6 acres and in one corner is a spring. In the 19th century "wakes" were held here on Trinity Sunday, tea was made with the spring water and a barrel of beer rolled up. From the camp walk south along the ridge path and down into the valley where you join the old Cardington Road. Turn right for Church Stretton.

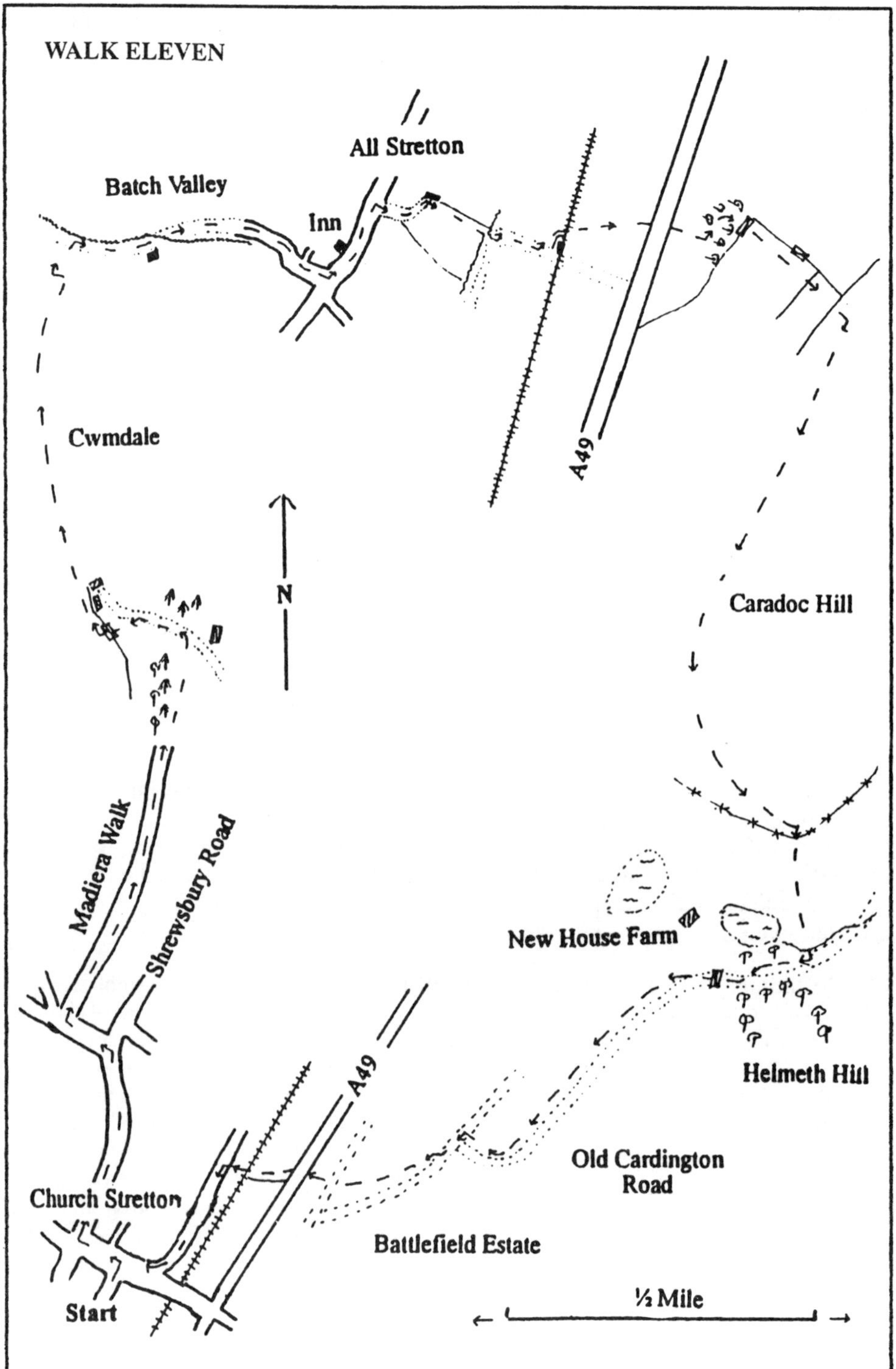
WALK ELEVEN
All Stretton
Batch Valley
Inn
Cwmdale
N
A49
Caradoc Hill
Madiera Walk
Shrewsbury Road
New House Farm
Helmeth Hill
A49
Old Cardington Road
Church Stretton
Battlefield Estate
Start
½ Mile

WALK ELEVEN ALL STRETTON/CARADOC 6 miles

This is not a duplication of walk 9 as it takes a different route on both outward and return legs. The outward stretch is on the western side of the Stretton vale and after crossing the vale at All Stretton you return along the lower slops of Caradoc with superb views.

START: Central Avenue (Pay and Display) Car Park.

DESCRIPTION: Leaving Church Stretton again by Madeira Walk you traverse Cwmdale this time to get to All Stretton, then a level walk across the valley floor to the western side of Caradoc and a return along the hillside with sumptuous views. Paths are dry, well defined and waymarked Good walking shoes perfectly adequate.

GRADE: Three

REFRESHMENTS: The Yew Tree Inn.

THE WALK: From the car park turn into Central Avenue then left into Sandford Avenue. Turn right at the Banks and walk along Shrewsbury Road. Turn first left into Carding Mill valley and then first right into Madeira Walk. At the end of Madeira Walk, turn left onto the track and crossing the cattle grid. At an open space on the left where the fence turns left uphill, leave the track and walk up until you pass through the fence and there turn right along a narrow path passing above and to the left of the cottages. By the stream turn right for All Stretton where turn left for the Yew Tree.

Pass the Inn and walk on for approximately 20 yards until opposite "Hall Cottage", cross the road and follow the public footpath, a wide track alongside a red brick wall which ends at "Meadgate Cottage". Go over the waymarked stile in front of the cottage and follow the hedge on your left. Crossing the stream by a footbridge turn left on another track. Shortly, ahead of you, is a railway crossing gate and a keepers cottage; don't go quite as far as the gate but seek a partially concealed stile, just after the telephone pole, and follow a footpath which, crossing behind the cottage garden, crosses the railway, and the field beyond, heading for a gap in the trees along the A49 road. Cross the road with care and go straight up the field opposite turning left up a slope into the woods on a well worn track. Continue ahead heading for Caradoc.

On crossing the second waymarked stile onto the slopes of Caradoc go straight up the hillside to the second footpath above you, and turn right. Stay on this path which gives superb views over the Stretton Vale as it gently rises and rounds the southern end of Caradoc until, turning again on to the eastern side you will see below you a waymarked stile. Now make your way into the valley and take care especially if the grass is wet. Turn right on the track crossing the stream by a footbridge and follow the well worn track through the gate and round the top edge of the field until you read the farm lane. On reaching the lane turn left along it as far as the "30" sign. Just beyond it, find a short flight of steps and a footpath sign at the top. Cross the field heading towards the electricity pylons. Cross the Roman Road "Watling Street" then the A49 and the railway. Bear right around "Windsor Place" and turn left for the town centre.

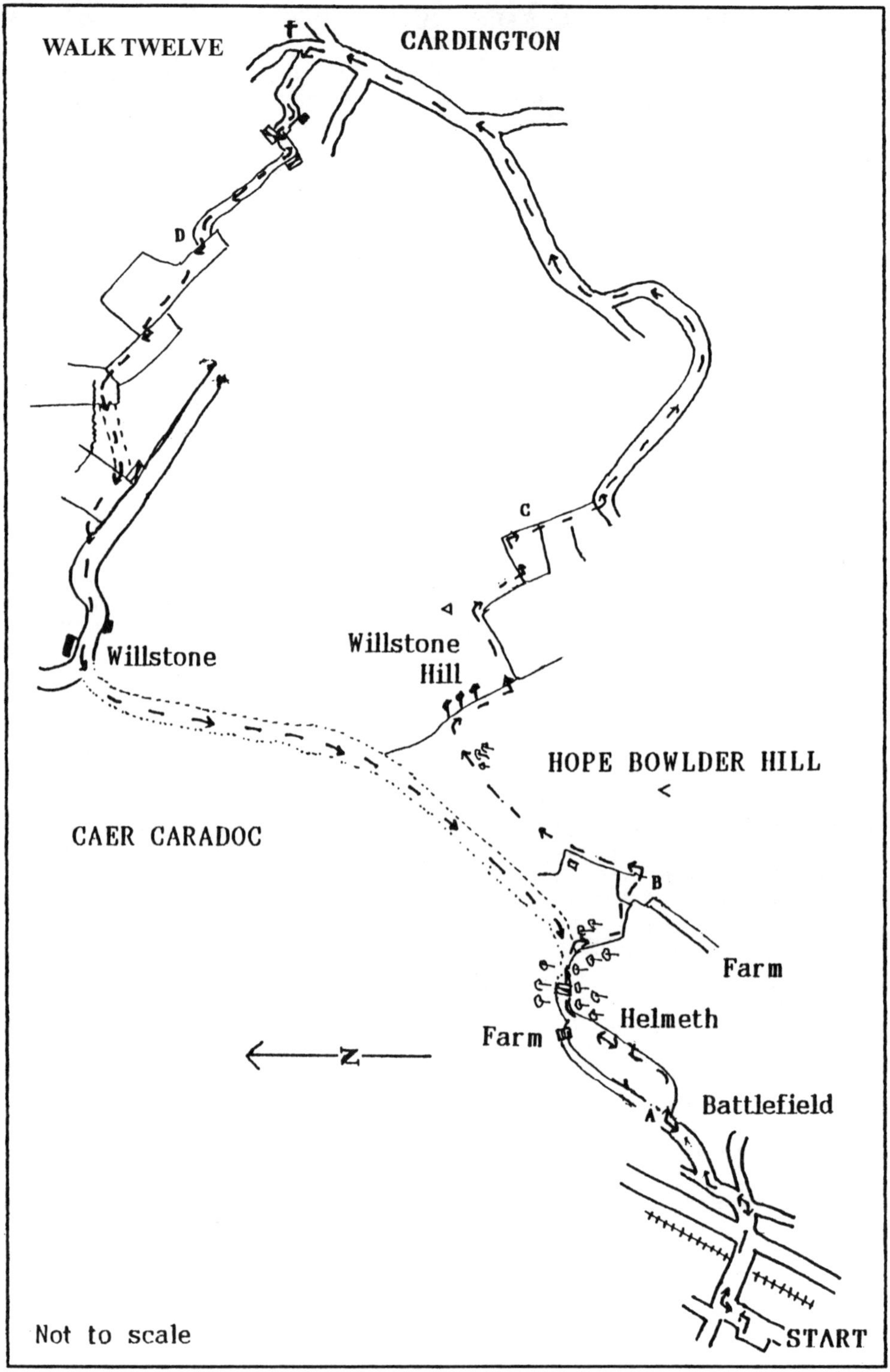
WALK TWELVE
CARDINGTON
D
C
Willstone
Willstone
Hill
HOPE BOWLDER HILL
CAER CARADOC
B
Farm
Helmeth
Farm
N
A
Battlefield
Not to scale
START

WALK TWELVE CARDINGTON 7 miles

This is an all day walk to one of Shropshire's prettiest villages. In season, Bluebells carpet the area behind and in Helmeth Wood which is open to the public.

START: Central Avenue(Pay & Display) Car Park

DESCRIPTION: At first in the valleys this walk soon changes to cross the line of hills to the east before descending into Cardington. The return walk follows the "Old Cardington Road".

GRADE: Five. Muddy areas in places so good shoes or boots are essential.

REFRESHMENTS:The Royal Oak Inn, for Lunches, and Grove Farm for teas.

THE WALK: From the car park turn left to Sandford Avenue then right and cross the railway. Go over the A49 road and turn left at the Catholic Church into Watling Street North. Fork right into a sunken lane alongside the Battlefield Estate. At (**A**)turn right at stile into field as signposted and keeping alongside the hedge you will be looking down into the sunken, and now very wet, "Old Cardington road". Go through gate at the end of the field with a small lake on your left and Helmeth Woods on your right. Shortly, ignore track going down left to cross stream, instead keep on the level for a few yards before turning right uphill to a metal kissing gate on the edge of the woods. Continue uphill alongside the woods until you get to the field at the top (**B**). Cross this field to the gate in top right-hand corner, go through onto the open hillside and turn left.

You are now on the lower slopes of Hope Bowdler Hill. Follow this path leaving the fields behind you. Look for a group of three trees ahead of you. Continue ahead until the path turns right and there is a short steep climb. At the top turn left over stile and follow fence along ridge until you can turn right, down hill, to the fields below. Go over stile into field and turn left as waymarked around edge of field to gate at (**C**)and go ahead over a stile and follow hedge(on left) until reaching lane. Turn left and follow lane to Cardington. Pass Grove Farm (teas) to the Church; the Royal Oak is behind the Church to the right.

From the pub return to the Church and turn right towards the telephone box and then left into a "No Through Road". Pass "The Old Vicarage" and turn left before field gate to follow a waymarked grassy lane to its end. Go over waymarked stile at (**D**)and head for far left corner of field. Go over waymarked stile there and turn right.

After the next waymarked stile, cross to a double stile at each end of a "sleeper" bridge and go up field as waymarked. Before lane turn slightly right to a stile in hedgerow and continue ahead across next field to facing stile the other side. Cross that stile for just a few yards to a final stile. Turn right in lane to Willstone. Turn off metalled road at Willstone onto dirt track to Caradoc and follow this right the way back to Church Stretton.

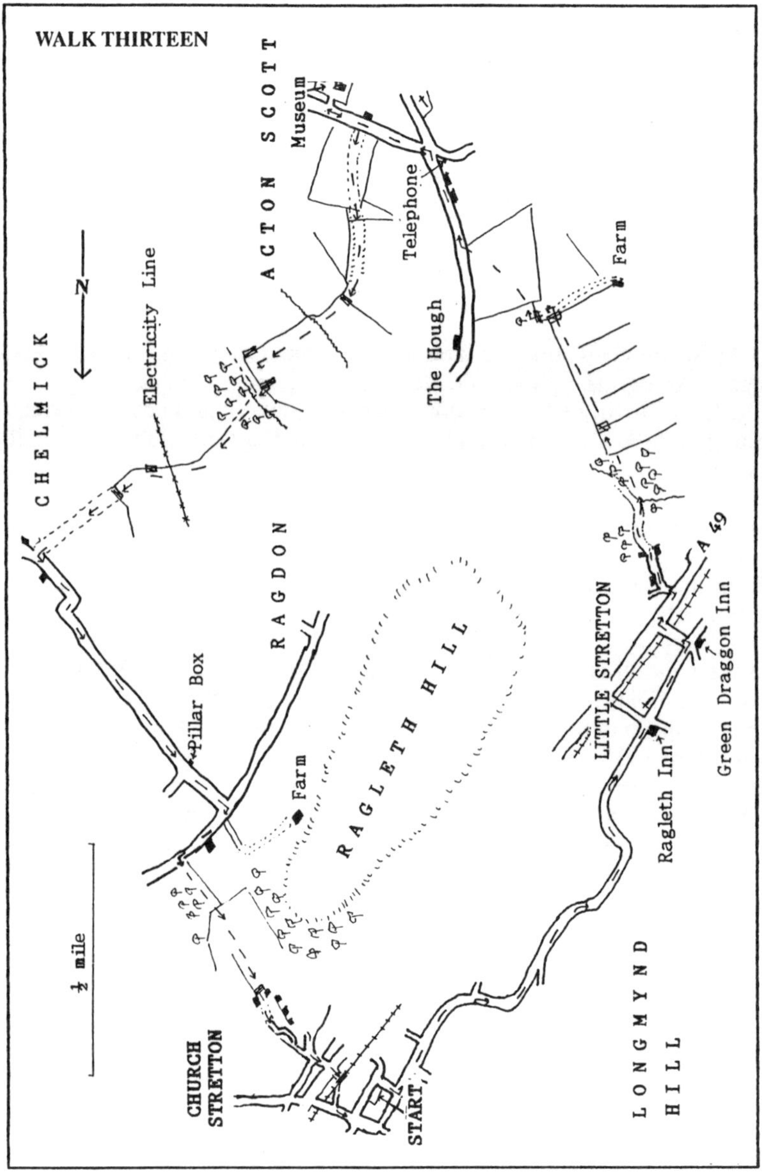

WALK THIRTEEN ACTON SCOTT 6 Miles

A particular delight for children is the working farm museum at Acton Scott. Run in the Victorian tradition it has a collection of rare animals and vintage farm machinery. Organic farm produce is on sale and a wide variety of attractions such as butter making, cider making, etc are held at week-ends throughout the year. Tel. 015946-306 to find out what's on or ask at the Information Centre.

START: Central Avenue Car Park or by bus to Little Stretton (The Green Dragon Inn) Bus runs every two hours.

GRADE:Two. An undulating walk with no difficult climbs. An easy walk across fields with well waymarked paths and good views. Good walking shoes or boots advisable.

REFRESHMENTS: Two Inn's at Little Stretton and hot & cold meals at Acton Scott Working Farm Museum.

THE WALK: Leave the car park for High Street(to the right of the supermarket) and turning left walk south along Ludlow Road to Little Stretton. Pass the "Ragleth Inn", the attractive half-timbered Church and, just opposite "The Green Dragon Inn", turn left into a narrow lane. Cross the A49 turning right for a few yards then turn left into a lane bearing right by the cottages. After the last house the track is grassy and climbs alongside a wood. At the top, and **before** a gate, turn right to a stile on top of the bank. Follow footpath through woods, over a footbridge, and out into fields beyond. Continue ahead through five fields(hedge on left). To your right the Long Mynd with, nearest, Ashes Valley, then going south, Callow Hollow, Minton Batch (with the state forest above it). At a field gate by a water trough turn left. Go through facing waymarked gate and turn right to a stile ahead, then half-left across the next field to the gate by a telephone post. Turn right in lane and turn left at cross roads by telephone box. The entrance to the Farm Museum is 100 yards farther on.

For the return walk, turn left out of the Museum back the way you came and go through the first waymarked gate on your right (opposite the entrance to Acton Scott farm). Follow track across field heading towards Ragleth Hill. In the corner of the field go over waymarked stile,through the wicket gate beyond, and walk for a short distance up a sunken track which emerges into a field giving superb views. Ragdon can be seen in the middle distance below Ragleth Hill. Continue ahead through next gate and down into a wooded gully where you cross a footbridge. Follow waymarks around three sides of this field to a wood.

Turn right into the woods and go uphill ignoring waymarked path to your right. Emerging from the woods follow the hedgerow, on your right, until by a hedged in grassy track you arrive at Chelmick. Turn left up the lane. Follow the lane passing the first "T" junction with a letter box by it and continue to the next "T" junction near a bungalow.

Turn right passing the entrance the "Dryhill Farm" on left. Continue along lane and turn next left at a signposted bridleway, a grassy track by an old quarry. The track drops down through the woods and by a stream emerges into a wide field. Pass the farm and join the lane continue down the track which ends at the Sandford Nursing Home. Cross the A49 and the railway to return to the town centre.

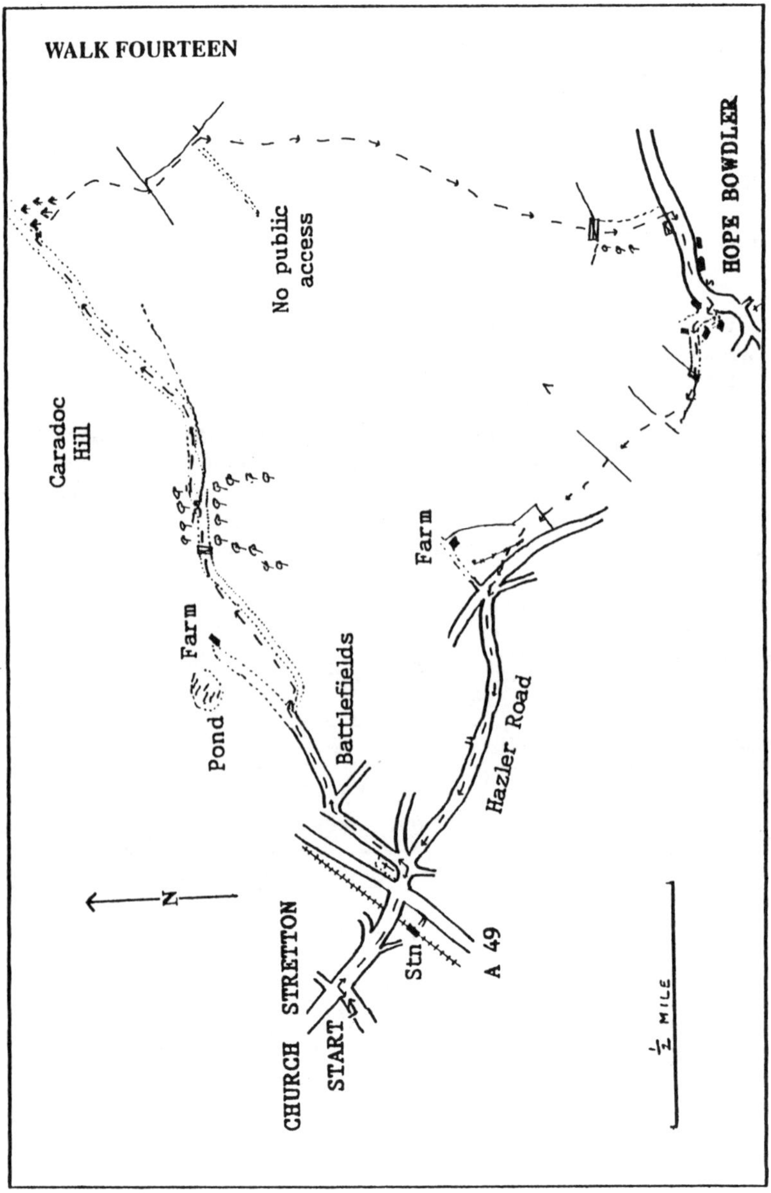

WALK FOURTEEN HOPE BOWDLER 5 miles

Apart from one short stretch on the return leg this walk is entirely devoid of road traffic and gives a superb view of Ape Dale as one traverses Hope Bowdler Hill

START: Central Avenue(Pay & Display) Car Park

GRADE: Three. A variable walk which can be muddy in isolated places. Good walking shoes or boots essential. Not too strenuous, only one short steep climb.

REFRESHMENTS: None.

THE WALK: From the car park turn left then right down Sandford Avenue and cross the railway. Cross the A49 by the traffic lights and turn left by the Roman Catholic Church along Watling Street North. At the entrance to the Battlefields Estate fork right into a deep lane with the houses above you to the right.

At the entrance to New House farm, turn right over a stile by the footpath sign and follow footpath around edge of field with the sunken "Cardington Road" below you to your right. This gradually rises to join your path at the end of the field when it then bears right through a gate and into a wooded area with Caradoc on your left and Helmeth Woods on your right. The area is a sea of bluebells in Spring.

Drop down left shortly and cross the stream by a footbridge and now follow a wide track which meanders up a gentle gradient for about a mile. At the top, by a small area of pine trees, turn right as waymarked "Ippikins Way" onto a grassy path which now heads towards Hope Bowdler Hill, leaving Caradoc directly behind you. Ippikin, so legend has it, was a twelfth century knight who, returning from the wars and finding that his services were not required, turned to stealing, a sort of early highwayman! Follow this path across an open grassy field, the path is not well worn but is sufficiently well used to be shown by the different shades of green. Once round the high ground drop down left to cross a flat area to a wicket gate and another "Ippikins Way" sign. Go through and bearing half-left follow the path through the ferns uphill onto the ridge of Hope Bowdler Hill.

At the top there is a waymarked stile on your left. Bear half-right away from it on a level grassy track(there is no footpath along the ridge). This path will shortly give one of the most exciting views in the area for as you walk the view gradually unfolds step by step until the whole valley is finally at your feet. Follow the track down hill and at the road turn right.

In the village pass the council houses and just beyond an "S" bend road sign, turn right onto a stoney track going uphill. In front of the facing house bear **LEFT** to a partially concealed waymarked stile to join a grassy track. After two more waymarked stiles a stream keeps you company. Continue in the same direction until a white bungalow comes into view directly ahead and two stiles further cross the last field,bearing half-left and keeping about 5 yards to the right of a wooden electricity pylon to join the main road by the bungalow. Cross over at the road junction and fork left into Hazler Road which drops down hill and back to the start.

WALK FIFTEEN

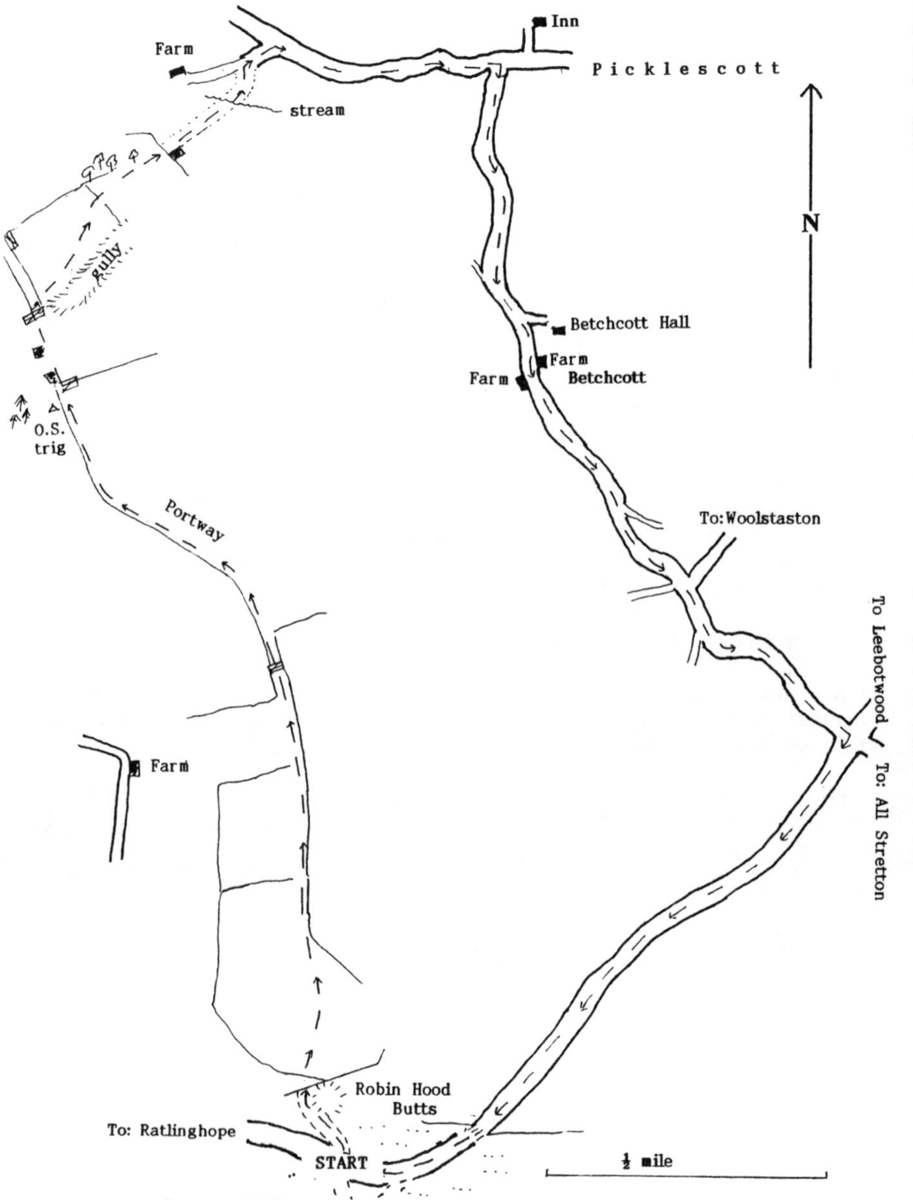

WALK FIFTEEN BETCHCOTT/PICKLESCOTT 5½ Miles

This easy walk commences by using "The Portway" a track of ancient Briton origin. After crossing fields the remainder of the walk is on quiet country lanes. The Inn at Picklescott is half way and well positioned for a welcome break.

START: High Park, 2 miles N.W. of Church Stretton.(O.S.Landranger 137, 435966)

GRADE: Two. Well defined tracks or country lanes and good underfoot for the most part. Good walking shoes adequate

REFRESHMENTS: The Bottle & Glass at Picklescott.

DESCRIPTION: Excellent views to north and south on the outward leg contrasts nicely with the neatly hedged lanes and fields of the return leg.

HOW TO GET THERE: from Church Stretton drive north to All Stretton; turn left at the telephone box signposted "Jinlye Guest House" then turn right and follow narrow lane uphill. After crossing open moorland continue to a cross roads. Turn left uphill as signposted "Ratlinghope" and after next cattle grid park on road side near the National Trust sign.

THE WALK: With your back to the cattle grid bear right down a wide track with a fence on the right hand side. Shortly after going through two facing gates the track bends gently right and at the third gate you join the exact line of "The Portway" an ancient track which runs the length of the Mynd north to south, it comes from behind you across the green field. Continue ahead still with the fence on your right. With Upper Darnford farm below to your left you come to two facing gates, go through the gate on the right marked with a large white arrow. For a few yards there is a fence to your left and right before the fence on the right terminates. About half a mile further, with a fence only on your left now, pass an Ordnance Survey Trig point and then a ruined barn. Go through facing gate and join a partially metalled track.

Go through the next facing gate and then turn right through a narrow "pedestrian" gate. Keep to the left of the gorse and skirting the gully on your right head half-left across the field towards a clump of trees by which is a redundant gate. With your back to the gate pass an isolated tree and a second isolated tree comes into view, you pass this and continue to the cottage. Go through the gate and join a rough track. On reaching the farm lane, turn right and then at the public lane turn right again.

At Picklescott turn right as signposted "Betchcott" (the signpost is ahead of you near the village green, completely out of alignment with the road!). For the Inn turn left at the green. Continue through Betchcott and follow the lane until you come to a cross roads. Turn right signposted "Ratlinghope" and so, return to your car.

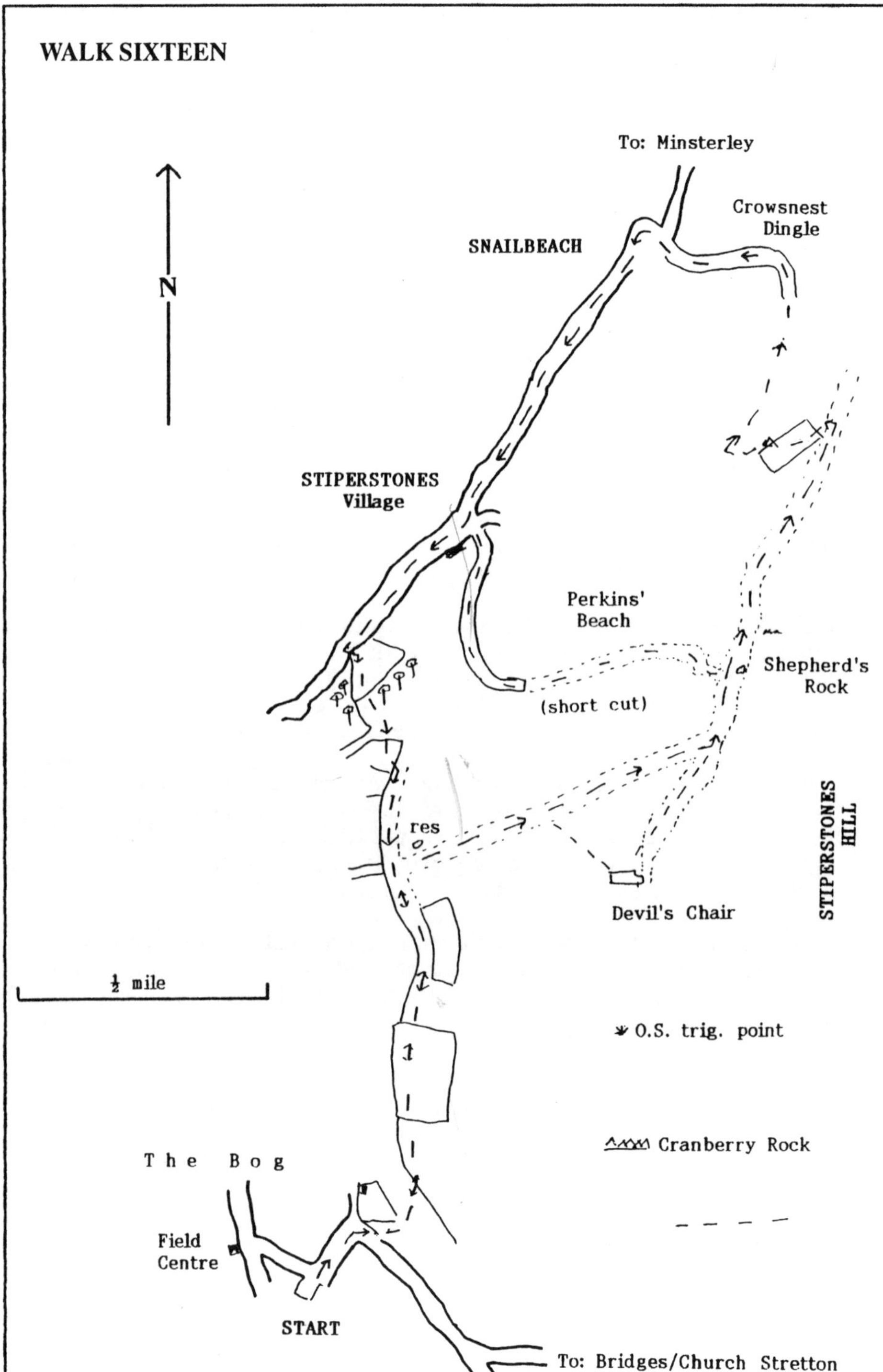
WALK SIXTEEN
N
To: Minsterley
Crowsnest
Dingle
SNAILBEACH
STIPERSTONES
Village
Perkins'
Beach
Shepherd's
Rock
(short cut)
res
Devil's Chair
STIPERSTONES
HILL
½ mile
O.S. trig. point
Cranberry Rock
The Bog
Field
Centre
START
To: Bridges/Church Stretton

WALK SIXTEEN THE STIPERSTONES 5 miles

The Stiperstones is a rocky hill to the west of Church Stretton. Deeply associated with "The Devil" the air of mystery and superstition which surrounds it is not enough to spoil its beauty especially in late Summer when the heather is in full bloom and the view, at any time of the year, is really something.

START: Free car park at "The Bog" (O.S.Map 137, 358979)

GRADE: Two. Fairly easy walking on well defined dry paths(apart from one boggy area near start) a slight climb on the way back. Good walking shoes adequate.

DESCRIPTION: The most striking feature of this hill is its heather which, unlike the Longmynd, is almost unfettered by bracken. This walk is best done in August when the heather is in full bloom. The views are superb in every direction.

REFRESHMENTS: The Stiperstones Inn, good bar meals and garden, and also a village shop. Teas and snacks at a cottage in Perkins Beach.

HOW TO GET THERE: Follow instructions in walk 5 as far as "The Horseshoes Inn", then, at the main road just beyond, turn left then immediately right signposted "The Bog". Follow the narrow lane directly towards the Stiperstones and after 1½ miles turn right. Just below the "Z" bend is a sizeable parking area on the site of a former lead mine.

LONE PINE CONNECTIONS: The Stiperstones features as the second most prominent area in the Lone Pine Books, no less than five stories being set in this region. Malcolm Saville did not describe the area is the exact detail he accorded to the Long Mynd but tried rather to "capture" the atmosphere of the area. Barton Beach is loosely modelled on "Stiperstones Village". From its geographical position, "Black Dingle" is Perkins Dingle, and "Greystones Dingle" is Crowsnest Dingle. There are no deep caves as described but some "tunnels" into the hillside do exist if you know where to find them. This was a very active mining area until a hundred years ago and remains of mine buildings still exist at Snailbeach. There is no farm in this area which equates to "Seven White Gates".

THE WALK: Walk back uphill as far as the "Z" bend, go over waymarked stile and continue upfield forking left to stile and an English Nature information board. Go over stile and follow path alongside the tumbled wall to your left. Go over two stiles after which the track then becomes wide and grassy.

By the next field gate near which, to your right, is a green fenced reservoir with fire-beaters outside, turn right on a wide well defined track. Ahead of you is the "Devil's Chair" the "cause célèbre" of the hills. If you wish to go up to it fork right when you see two parallel paths heading directly in that direction, otherwise continue and turn left along the wide flat track, where the path from the chair rejoins. Walk north away from the chair.

The next junction of paths just below "Shepherd's Rock"is marked with a cairn of stones and if you wish to shorten the walk you can turn left down "Perkins Beach" directly to Stiperstones Village, otherwise continue along the top as far as the field. It seems strange to find a grassy field up here surrounded by heather. It is known as "Blakemoorflat" and was cultivated when Squatters built their homesteads here. Probably employees at the Snailbeach Mines they would have found the fresh air and tranquility a welcome change to the smoke, dirt and noise of the industrial environment in which they worked. When you get there turn left off the main track and then left again through the gate. Go straight ahead across the field heading for the line of trees, almost doubling back on yourself. Through the line of tress turn right and find a stile in the lower area of the field. Turn left over the stile. With the fence on your left go as far as the fourth fence post where fork right onto an almost unseen and very narrow path through the heather. As a direction guide you will see, in the distance, a hill surmounted by a head of trees, you should head straight for it. The path becomes clearer after a few yards. At the head of the valley below and unseen at first is a stand of "fire-beaters", go down to it and then turn right on a clear path down into Crowsnest Dingle.

At the road turn left and walk back to Stiperstones Village. Continue through the village and on leaving the houses behind watch for the word "slow" painted on the road for oncoming traffic. At the top of the bank on your immediate left is a waymarked stile, cross it and turn right uphill keeping alongside the fence. Ignore the next stile across the field to your left, but carry on uphill until you come to a second waymarked stile. Continuing uphill, ignore a path on the right, until you come to a field and a stile. Cross the stile and field to a gate in the far left-hand corner. Turn right along the track and back to the start.

WALK SEVENTEEN MUCH WENLOCK 3/4 miles

This walk takes in the countryside around Much Wenlock famed for its Abbey, which is well worth a visit as also is the Parish Church.

START: Public(Pay & Display) Car Park in the centre of the town.

GRADE: Two.

REFRESHMENTS: none on the walk. Many pubs and a "chippy" in High Street, there is also a "Spar" which can be found on the approach to the Abbey. Ask any local for directions

HOW TO GET THERE: From Church Stretton drive east on the B4371 as signposted "Much Wenlock". On reaching the A458 turn right as for "Bridgnorth" and then, by the Gaskell Arms Hotel the road swings right, still as for Bridgnorth. After the filling station turn left for the car park. From Shrewsbury take the A458, then as above.

DESCRIPTION: Easy walking on level ground and crossing arable fields. In wet weather Wellington Boots or walking boots strongly advised as one gateway doubles as the bed of a stream!

THE WALK: Leave the car park by "Burgage"towards the "No entry" sign and turn left down a narrow passage with the sign "Cycling Prohibited" emerging through an archway into High Street opposite the H.S.B.C Bank. Turn left.

Pass the Post Office, Talbot Inn and Barclays Bank all on the left and walk west, out of the town, as far as the main road with the "Gaskell Arms"on the opposite corner, here turn right into "Smithfield Road" signed "A4169 Ironbridge/Telford". Pass the Police Station and then, on the opposite side of the road, the fire station, here cross the road and walk up "Bridge Road". Cross the old railway bridge but the cutting has been filled in now and no trace of the former line remains. At "Southfield Road" go straight ahead towards a copse by way of a rough track.

At the junction of paths, on the edge of the copse, fork right onto a path which runs along the edge of the copse with the field hedge on your right. In a short while the path swings left and you emerge into a field. Continue ahead, down the field, with the hedge on your right. At the bottom corner of the field go through a narrow iron wicket gate, it is here the stream may be encountered using the same track. *(For shorter walk, walk straight ahead until you reach Edge wood, see dotted line on map). Otherwise, turn left.*

Follow the hedge, with the drainage ditch on your left, through this field and the next field. Towards the end of the second field, bear slightly left to cross into the adjacent field through a wide gap, there is a public footpath sign in the hedge. The path, here, changes sides, and whereas the hedge was on your

WALK SEVENTEEN

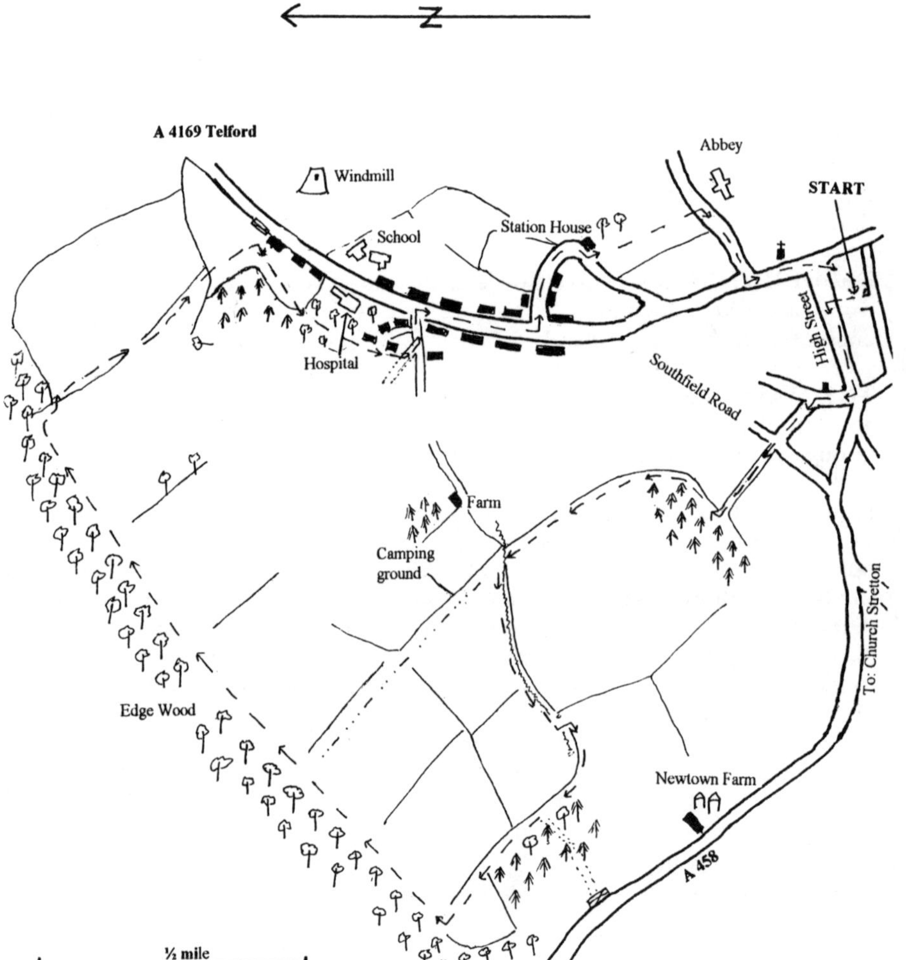

left, from here on it is on your right. Follow the hedge round to the right. The path now runs between the edge of the copse and the hedge. This stretch may be difficult in summer due to nettles so find a way through the woods. Half-way up the slope cross a wide forest track and continue uphill as waymarked until you emerge into a field at the top. Continue ahead until you reach "Edge Wood" and a waymark post at a junction of paths. Turn right.

Now walk along the field path, with Edge Wood on your left, through two fields. *At the end of the second field the short cut joins.* Ahead of you now you will see the pink cooling towers of the Buildwas Power Station. Eventually,after three more fields the path drops down a slope and bends to the right as the Edge Woods spread "inland". Find the stile, a little down to the left and cross through the end of the woods into the adjacent field, turning right. The path now continues, with hedge on your right for a short distance before bearing slightly right to run alongside another hedge now on your left. Go over the next stile and walk down the field towards the street lamp and "30" signs. The base of an old windmill can be seen above the trees ahead.

Cross the road and turn right. Pass the School and the Hospital and at the "P Coaches" sign, turn left into Station Road. The old windmill base can again be seen on top of its hill, before arriving at the old Station, now a private dwelling. Pass the station and turn left crossing the old track bed and find the stile in the corner by the garden fence. Cross stile and go straight across the field emerging onto a metalled lane at the Abbey car park. Turn right. At the main street, by Spar, turn left. Pass the church and the Market Hall and cross the road by the clock tower. Heading through an archway by "Wenlock Fine Arts" turn right to the car park.

Carding Mill Valley

WALK EIGHTEEN

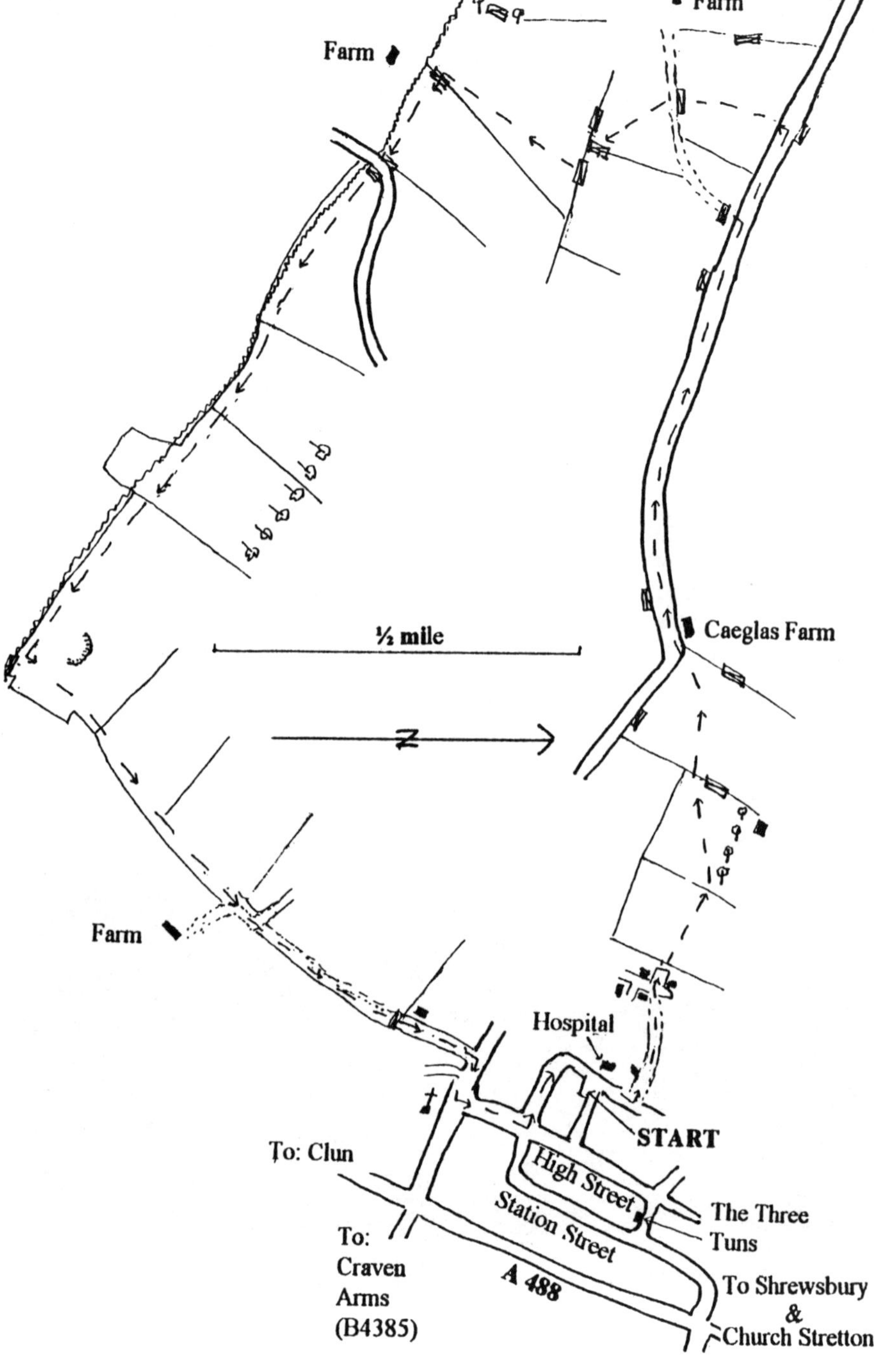

WALK EIGHTEEN BISHOP'S CASTLE 3½ miles

This walk takes in the countryside to the west of Bishop's Castle which was once a "rotten borough" and the smallest borough in England. The town itself is well worth spending time walking round, at the top of High Street is the old town hall on stilts and also the market hall.

START: Public Car Park (free) in Harley Jenkins Street.

GRADE: Two.

REFRESHMENTS: Pubs, cafés and a "chippy" in Bishop's Castle.

HOW TO GET THERE: From Church Stretton drive south on the A49 and turn right onto the B4370 at the Marshbrook filling station signposted "Bishop's Castle" and continue to follow the "Bishop's Castle" signs. From Shrewsbury take the A488.

DESCRIPTION: Easy walking through fields and well waymarked throughout. Walking boots or good stout shoes usually sufficient.

LONE PINE CONNECTIONS: Bishop's Castle figures prominently in several Lone Pine books. In "Lone Pine Five" it was here that the story starts with the discovery of a Roman christening spoon at an auction sale. In "Neglected Mountain" the children came here for the fair. In "Home to Witchend" it was at the market the twins discovered Miss Ballanger doing sketches.

THE WALK: Turn left out of the car park then right into Union Street passing the hospital on the left. A little way up Union Street is an attractive row of cottages one of which is called "The Smithy". Just beyond, by a cottage with a water hydrant plate on the wall saying 3/16, turn left into Laburnum Alley. Follow this path past a house called "Highfields" and then with a high brick wall on your left and a holly hedge on your right come to a wicket gate. Go through and following a path of lose chippings to the housing estate road. Turn left. Almost immediately, by number 73, turn right into a cul-de-sac at the end of which is a waymarked stile.

Go straight ahead in the first field, the next stile cannot be seen at first because of the rising ground. Go over next stile and be warned that the waymark arrow is not quite correct as the path bears slightly to the left, away from the line of scrubby trees. Aim for a point to the left of the field gate in the far hedgerow where there is a stile. Go over that stile and continue ahead along the bottom of the field turning left up the slope when almost at the end of the field and by a waymarked stile in the top corner gain access to the lane.

Go straight ahead up the lane. After a mile you come to a public footpath sign on the left, at the top of a short bank, there is also another signpost over the road opposite. Go over a double stile into a field and ahead straight down the middle of the field to a distant field gate. It is waymarked but you won't be able to see it, unless you have binoculars, until nearly there. Away to your left the Long Mynd straddles the horizon while nearer you can see the Vodophone transmitter on Oakeley Mynd. Go through gate, cross farm track and head off across field towards a gate in the far corner, there is a fence away to your left.

At the corner of the field are two gates, one facing and one to the left with waymarks on it. Go through the latter and then immediately turn right through a second waymarked gate. Now strike out dead ahead, leaving the gate behind you, and heading towards the left-hand edge of a distant pine wood. The hedge on the left gradually nears as you drop down a slope to a stream in the valley bottom. Turn left through a field gate and thence into a lane.

Here, if you wish to shorten the walk, you can return to Bishop's Castle by turning left and walking back along the lane, otherwise, cross the lane and waymarked stile joining "The Shropshire Way". Now walk ahead, keeping the stream, on your right, through five fields, with either stiles or gates or both, and usually waymarked. At the end of the last field, after passing, on your left, an old quarry, turn left up the hill to find a stile in the top corner, there are two corners, so go to the second, then,with the hedge on your right, walk straight on joining, in the second field a farm track for a short way. When the farm track turns left continue ahead on a grassy track hedged in on both sides and thus, passing through the front garden of Fields' Cottage, follow the track back to the town. Passing the fire station, turn right then left for Church Street, and then, past the garage, left again for the car park.

Looking North From Caradoc

WALK NINETEEN OFFA'S DYKE (CLUN) 6 miles

This walk takes in the countryside around Clun, featured in Malcolm Saville's book "The Secret of Grey Walls". This is wide open sheep country with rolling green hills and it can be quite rough on a windy day on the Dyke.

START: At the approach to Burfield Farm,(O.S.Map 137,262804) 2 miles from Clun.

GRADE: Three. Easy walking, mostly on tracks with only a couple of fields to cross on the return leg. Although the countryside is hilly the gradients are easy.

REFRESHMENTS: Tea,Coffee and cakes at Mrs.Thomas's, Garbett Villa (Tel: 01547 528696). Pubs in Clun.

HOW TO GET THERE: From Church Stretton drive south on the A49 to Craven Arms where you turn right onto the B4368 for Clun. In Clun fork left "A488 Knighton". After crossing the bridge go ahead and about 100 yards after passing the Church, fork right signed "Springhill/Anchor". After passing a farm which straddles the road there is a wide grassy verge on the right. Park just before the cross roads with a signpost "Springhill/Anchor".

DESCRIPTION: Superb views from Offa's Dyke, more details in the text. This country abounds with Skylarks and Buzzards.

LONE PINE CONNECTIONS: "The Secret of Grey Walls" was the fourth book in the series and concerned sheep stealing in this area, the stolen sheep were concealed in the Offa's Dyke ditch before being transported away in furniture vans. The house called "Grey Walls" was the hideout for the rustlers and "Bury Fields" one of the farms from which the sheep were stolen, are both passed on this walk.

THE WALK: From the car, turn right then turn left as signposted to "Burfield Farm" marked with a bridleway sign and a "Jack Mytton Way" waymarker. The farm is about a mile from the road along a winding farm track.

Burfield Farm is the "Bury Fields" in the book. At the farm go straight ahead,with the farmhouse to your left and a barn to your right, there are waymark signs, to a facing field gate. Follow the track as far as a "T" junction of tracks. Turn left here, cross the stream by a concrete bridge, and continue to follow the track through two facing gates, both waymarked. As a roadside telephone post comes into view you will pass through Offa's Dyke for the first time. Continue on the farm track to the lane, and turn left, not forgetting to close the gate.

WALK NINETEEN

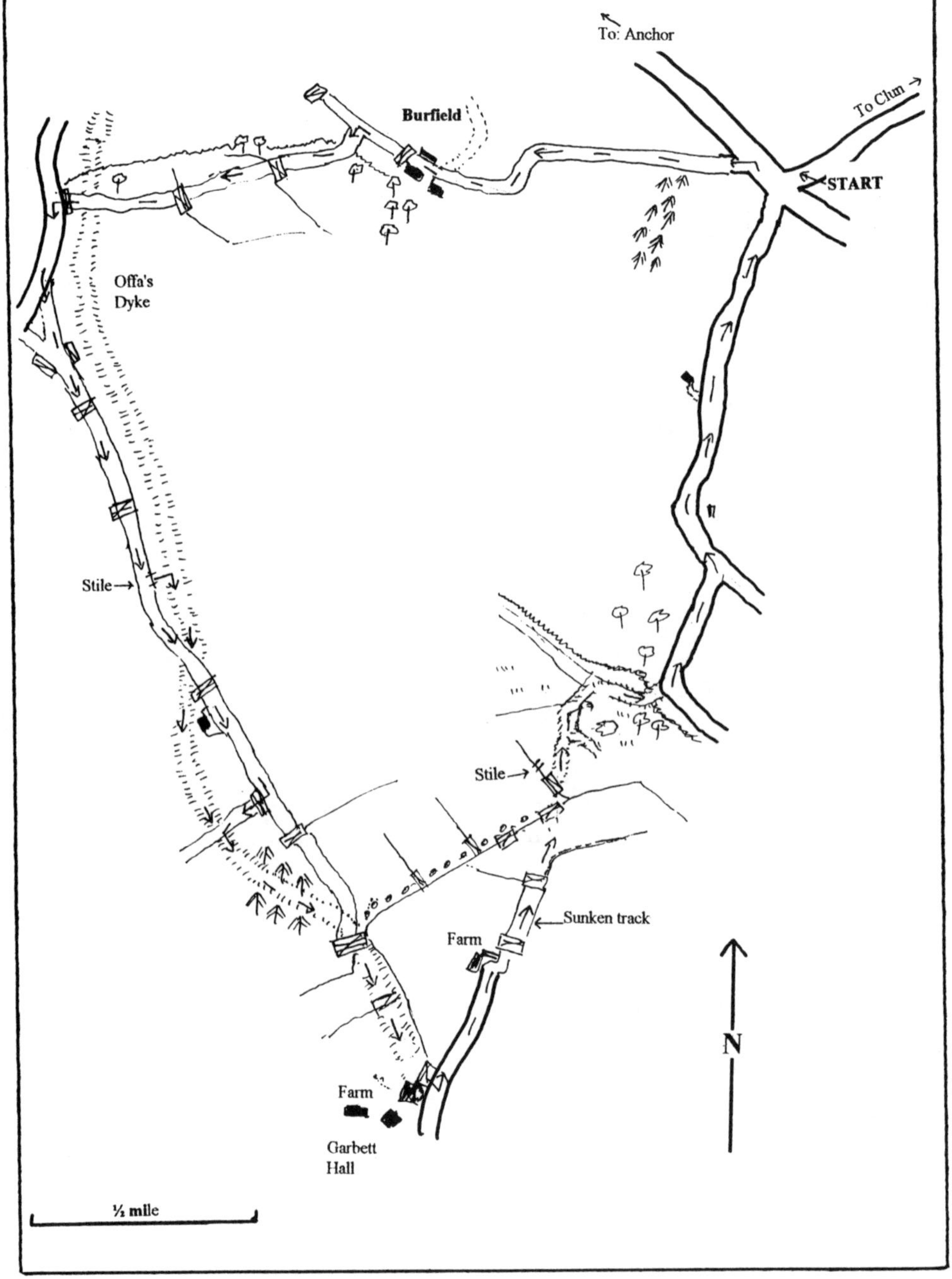

Walk along the lane for about a hundred yards, with Offa's Dyke on the left. Where the road bears right, fork left onto a grassy track by the "Offa's Dyke" signpost and continue ahead with a fence on your left and an area of bracken on your right. You will shortly join a new track which comes in from your right.

Walk on now on the farm track through three facing gates, some of them marked with the Offa's Dyke acorn sign. Ahead of you, in the near distance, is the hilly bulk of "Radnor Forest". Offa's Dyke gets closer now and eventually you will see a stile on your left marked with the acorn. You can either climb over now and walk along the dyke or stick to the track, the track is easier on the feet! If you elect to walk the dyke just follow the acorn signs on the stiles. If you keep to the track follow it until after passing a dutch barn on your right the track swings right through a facing gate marked with "Jack Mytton Way" signs. Go through and now turn left along the actual dyke. The dyke drops steeply downhill through an area of Pine trees planted on the dyke itself. In the far distance, to the south, you can now see the Black Mountains. Rejoin the track at a facing gate at the bottom of the hill.

If you wish to shorten the walk, turn left here and keeping the hedge on your right walk ahead through three fields until you come to a waymarked stile to the left of a field gate, here the longer walk will join. *Now jump two paragraphs.*

To continue the main walk - go through facing gate and continue to follow the track and as you drop down through clumps of gorse bushes Garbett Hall suddenly comes into view. Although nothing like "Grey Walls" as described in the book, the gabled windows, the grey roof and walls its location and sudden appearance, all contribute to this being the inspiration behind the fictional property. Pass to the back left of the house and out into the lane. Turn left. If Mrs Thomas is open for refreshments there will be "open" signs here.

Follow lane, passing Garbett Villa. The lane ends at another farm. Go straight ahead through the farmyard and make for a facing field gate to the right of a barn. Go straight ahead up the sunken track but if it is waterlogged walk along the edge of the field near the ditch. At the top of the field you have to drop back into the ditch which, hopefully, is not so wet now, to pass through a facing gate. The track peters out in the field as the slope levels off. Ahead is a hedge across the top of the field. Bear half-right making for an as yet unseen gate in the far right-hand corner of the field, and as you breast the rise it will come into view. Go through and turn right to another gate to the left of which is a waymarked stile.

Go over stile and follow, slightly left, a grassy track with a shallow bank on its right side. This takes you down to a farm track. Turn left down hill following the track to the lane. Turn left along the lane back to the start.

WALK TWENTY

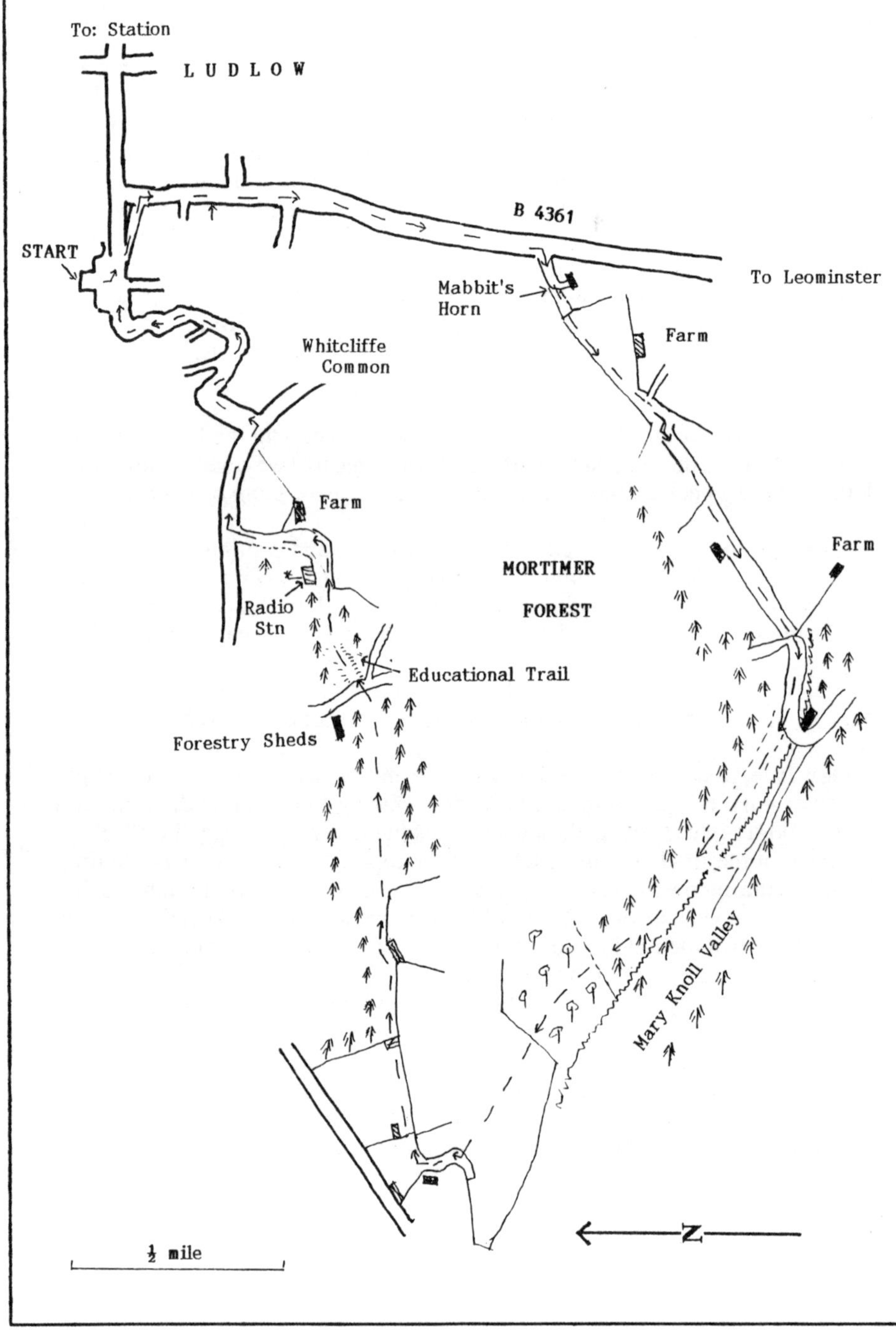
To: Station
LUDLOW
B 4361
START
Mabbit's Horn
To Leominster
Farm
Whitcliffe Common
Farm
MORTIMER FOREST
Farm
Radio Stn
Educational Trail
Forestry Sheds
Mary Knoll Valley
½ mile
N

Ludlow is one of our finest market towns containing a wealth of architectural delights. It is worth a walk in itself and the Information Centre in Market square will be pleased to help. Broad Street has been described as "one of the most memorable streets in England" the steep yet spacious street with its cobbled "banks" leads through the 13th century "Broad Gate" to Ludford Bridge. Ludlow has close associations with the poet A.E.Houseman and more recently featured in the BBC TV series "Blot on the Landscape".

START:Market Place Car Park

GRADE: Three. Being on clay, mud is a problem in wet weather. The minor changes in gradient are not too demanding. Good walking shoes are fine in good weather, but in wet weather Wellington boots or walking boots are best as the clay can be slippery.

REFRESHMENTS: Various Inns, cafe's and restaurants in Ludlow. Strongly recommend DeGray's in Broad Street.

DESCRIPTION: After traversing the famous "Broad Street" you walk south along the B4361 road until turning off towards Mortimer Forest. Noted for its population of Roe Deer the forest covers 8400 acres. In the upper part of Mary Knoll Valley is a small area of private deciduous woodland kept as a Nature Reserve. There are good views on the outward legs but especially on the last lap of the return when you stand on Whitcliffe Common with Ludlow spread out before you.

PARKING - public car park behind the Kwick-Save Supermarket in the Market Square. Most street parking is limited to one hour. If you come by train walk uphill,left, from the station and turn right at the top "Gravel Hill" and continue straight ahead to the Castle and the Market Square.

LONE PINE CONNECTIONS: Ludlow is mentioned in several books but plays an important part in , "Secret of the Gorge", and "Strangers at Witchend". Readers of Malcolm Saville's Buckingham series will remember the title "Master of Maryknoll" and on this walk you walk the valley and pass the house in which the story was set.

THE WALK: From the car park, cross the Market Square to Woolworths and walk along the narrow passage. Turn right down Broad Street. Note the old arched gateway the only surviving example.

Cross Ludford Bridge by the Charlton Arms Hotel. Just beyond this note the plaque in front of the rock face, partially concealed by the memorial seat. Walk along the road for a ½ mile to the entrance to "Mabbit's Horn". Turn right up the drive.

Go straight ahead at gate to house to a field gate at the end of a hedged in passage. Over waymarked stile and continue ahead with at first a fence, then a stone wall, on your right. A deep gully, beyond the fence, is joined at the end of the field. Carry straight on as waymarked, ignore the track leading to the farmhouse, and shortly bear right(also waymarked) in a wide triangular area towards field but then bear left staying on the green lane. At first hedged in on both sides the lane soon becomes hedged on the left side only. Go ahead at facing gate with waymarked stile and at end of field pass in front of the cottage to join a well defined track which leads into the forest at a high metal gate.

On entering the forest take the track going **down** hill, waymarked now with a blue arrow, as far as a sweeping bend by a cottage. Fork right now onto a narrow path indicated by a Forestry Commission post marked with a green ring. This is Mary Knoll Valley and you keep the stream on your left, ***never*** cross it. After approximately ¼ mile the track again sweeps round a wide left-hand bend to cross over the stream, and here you leave it to join a new narrower track which joins in front of you at the bend. As mentioned before, do not cross the stream it **must** stay on your left.

The track is a little steeper here and then leaves the Forestry Commission wood to enter the Mary Knoll Nature Reserve. Continue ahead and cross the field by the well defined grassy track. This is usually a good place for Deer. At the top of the field, go through the gate and turn right uphill on a new track. Passing the house and over stile by gate, turn right then right again to pass to the right of a barn and follow the sunken track up the side of the field with the hedge on your right. Go through the gate and into the woods.

After passing a small extinct quarry on your right bear left at the field gate staying on the level track just inside the woods. You now stay on this track right through the woods. In places it is quite deep and must have been used for centuries. After another ½ mile cross the Forestry Commission road near to some buildings and continue ahead on the sunken track passing the "Educational Trail" notice. Shortly you will be on the edge of the forest again with fields on your right. Just after passing the Forestry Commission radio transmitter the path turns left downhill, and narrows, to emerge on the main road. Turn right. At the first turning left by the "Z" bend sign, turn left and follow the road downhill and back to Ludlow.